Hunting High Country Mule Deer

by Mike Eastman

Library of Congress Catalog Number: 95-94687

ISBN Number 0-9657704-0-0

First Printing May 1997
Second Printing May 1999
Third Printing June 2001
Fourth Printing October 2003
Fifth Printing November 2004

Printed in Canada

Cover photo by: Mark McCord
Illustrations: Chris Lacey
Guy Eastman

Photo on inside front cover: Mike Eastman in the early 70s guiding trophy mule deer hunters above timberline in Jackson Hole, Wyoming. *Photographer unknown.*

MHE Ventures
P. O. Box 798, Powell, WY 82435
Phone: (307) 754-5584

Dedication

I want to dedicate this book to my father who instilled in me the love of hunting mule deer at a very early age. Also Uncle Billy Kolhs who took the time to take me into the back country when I was very young to hunt trophy mule deer. To all dedicated hunters who have endured the elements to pursue trophy mule deer.

In 1967, Mike at 19 years of age guided a hunter to this trophy six-point bull while working for Keith Stilson, an old time Jackson Hole outfitter.

About the Author

Mike Eastman grew up in Jackson Hole, Wyoming, where the observation and pursuit of mule deer occupied most of his waking hours for over 35 years. He is the oldest son of the late Gordon Eastman who was considered the best producer of outdoor films in the industry. Mike grew up filming and working on such classic hunting videos as Mule Deer Hunters, Rocky Mountain Safari Elk, Rocky Mountain Safari Deer, Talk to the Elk, Mule Deer Action and Bowhunting Record Mule Deer.

As a youth, Mike could most often be found watching or hunting the high country mule deer of western Wyoming. This area supports perhaps the finest mule deer gene pool in the world. Later, he was able to turn his love of these great deer into a profession as for many years he outfitted trophy mule deer hunters in the high country around Jackson Hole.

In 1987 Mike launched the trophy hunting magazine, *The Eastmans' Journal*, a guide for big game hunting in the Rocky Mountain states. The publication covers hunting strategies, trophy areas, outfitters and includes great stories from successful trophy hunters. In just 10 years, *The Journal* has grown into an internationally distributed magazine that is regarded by many as the best source for western hunting information ever produced. Mike has also filmed, produced and marketed his own video library that includes the popular Mule Deer Stalker series.

A noted author and lecturer, Mike has spoken at many national shows and travels across the country presenting his own mule deer seminars to sellout crowds each year.

Mike, a longtime advocate of "fair chase" hunting practices, is respected throughout the hunting world for his knowledge of wildlife behavior. Hunter, publisher, film maker, author and lecturer; Mike Eastman has done it all.

Mike Eastman at age seven in Washington state with his first deer. Also pictured is Mike's father, Gordon, and brother, Brad.

This 31-inch buck that was living in a scrub pine patch was taken by Mike in a high mountain basin.

Table of Contents

Foreword 11

Section I - Research

1. The Four Year Plan 17
2. Finding An Area 21
3. Scouting 25

Section II - Tactics

4. Coyoting Out 33
5. Glassing 67
6. Early Fall Hunting 77
7. Mid-Fall Hunting 91
8. Pockets and Slides 97
9. Mule Deer Behavior 119

Section III - Judging

10. Introduction To Field Judging 127
11. Trash Factor Buck 129
12. Rack Bracketing 133
13. Spread 141
14. Good Fronts Make Up For Bad Backs 149
15. Good Back Tines 159
16. Eye Guards 163
17. Mass 165

Section IV - Trophy Bucks

18. Trophy Bucks 171
19. Future of High Mountain Mule Deer Hunting 185

Section V - Areas

20. High Country Areas 189

Foreword

Some people may ridicule you for trophy hunting. They might say trophy hunting isn't a good reason to be outdoors. I have a burning desire to hunt and experience the wilderness. My reply to those people is, "name one sport or activity in which American males don't keep score." It's just a way of grading our activities.

Hunting the high country gets in your blood. There's something about watching a 30-inch mulie bounce along a 10,000-foot ridge with nothing except deep blue sky between the tines of his rack. Visions like these engrave themselves into the trophy hunter's memory of stone.

Some hunters make collecting just a single trophy mule deer at this altitude the quest of a lifetime. Many consider it to be the number one trophy hunting challenge in all the West. This type of hunting is tough and requires the very best physical conditioning.

Because you can't grow mule deer in compounds or pens like you can elk and whitetail, they have suddenly become one of the most highly sought after trophies in all of North America. Hunters with enough money can always buy a chance to hunt a big buck on a private ranch while the rest of us are thrown into hunting areas on public land. There, our only chance at a large buck is to find him in his hidey-hole. I know I'm in his terrain and the odds are in his favor. Personally, I prefer this type of hunting. I find great satisfaction in doing my own research and experiencing the exhilaration of a one-on-one challenge with a smart big buck.

During the 60s, hunting methods were much different from today. The seasons were more liberal...you never hunted mule deer until after Thanksgiving and seasons were often open until Christmas. In some areas you could harvest two or three bucks in a single season. My brothers and I would take our old 4-wheel drive truck, slap on the chains, and travel down through the desert country where the mule deer wintered. We would drive around glassing bucks until we located the one we wanted, then attempt a stalk. We saw many good trophy mule deer in those years and took some outstanding bucks as well. In fact, there were so many that we took it for granted. We thought everyone had hunting like that.

This type of game management lasted only four or five years more until several bad winters coupled with overkill from too many multiple deer licenses severely depleted our mule deer herds. The entire game population in the mountains of Wyoming, Colorado and Idaho suffered substantial loses.

When the hunting regulations changed, our tactics had to change as well. The seasons were shortened and we were forced to hunt mule deer much earlier in the fall. Because they could no longer be hunted on their winter ranges late in the year, we had to learn to hunt them in the high country.

I have spent over 40 years hunting above tree line for mule deer in Colorado, Idaho and my home state of Wyoming. I have learned the ways of the high country and the habits of the bucks that live there. It wasn't easy, but after years of hard work and dedication it all paid off.

Now as publisher of *The Eastmans' Journal*, I talk to thousands of hunters every year who are trying to collect a trophy mule deer. Most are looking for an easy answer. They jump from one hot area to another frantically hunting every high profile unit they can in search of their dream buck.

It's partially a problem of America's mindset today. We decide to buy a new $25,000 truck and we can be on the road enjoying it in a mere two hours. However, it's not that easy to take a trophy mule deer. It requires long hours of investigative work to first find a good area. Then it takes several years to learn the habits and behavioral patterns of the trophy bucks in that area.

Most people have a difficult time dealing with the mental aspect of trophy hunting. For the impatient person it's hard to adjust to the fact that one day you may see a good deer, then spend years waiting and watching before you see another. After years of interviewing successful trophy hunters with impressive collections of mule deer, I have discovered their best bucks usually came from areas where the terrain was very similar. It could be the oak-brush country, the cedar breaks, or in my case high mountain peaks above 9,500 feet.

I have written this book for the hunter who specifically wants to hunt in the high country. It will give you solid information on becoming a self-made trophy mule deer hunter. There is no surefire solution, but with a long-term game plan you can acquire the needed edge to become proficient at hunting mule deer in the high country.

Mike Eastman
Publisher/Senior Editor
The Eastmans' Journal

Photo by Carl Oksanen

Section I

RESEARCH

1-1: Laverne Caldeira took my advice and used llamas to get into remote mountain areas that hold trophy bucks.

Chapter 1

The Four Year Plan

The road to harvesting a good trophy mule deer can be a long, rough haul. With this in mind it is very important that you assemble a game plan. Many hunters have difficulty drawing permits because they only apply for high profile areas throughout the West. After a few years of not drawing any permits, they become discouraged and often times resentful. Some give up mule deer hunting all together. I know of many areas that contain substantial populations of 170 to 180 class trophy bucks. They do, however, lack 200-inch bucks beneath every tree. With a little research you can find these little known areas and hunt 170 B&C class bucks every fall.

I have developed a system over the years that will allow you to consistently hunt in a favorable area for trophy bucks, year after year. This four year program is the strategy of the '90s. The plan I will outline should be modified for your own use. Its purpose is to give you a starting point and help you to remain focused. It's like anything else, if you don't have a plan you will continually find yourself sidetracked from your goal.

Too many hunters jump from area to area without ever getting to know how to hunt the country most effectively. Some may draw a permit for a hard-to-draw area and have only one season or one week for that matter to attempt to learn the movements of the deer before the season opens. I have found that most truly successful trophy mule deer hunters hunt the same country year after year. To give you a case in point, the Kaibab is hunted by Arizona residents and nonresidents alike, however 95 percent of the quality bucks taken are by the repeat resident hunters. These hunters are able to hunt the same area over and over until the country and behavior patterns of the deer are mastered. This leaves most outsiders to wander aimlessly throughout the area in a futile attempt at stumbling upon a smart old buck.

It's like anything else, you need a well devised and carefully implemented plan of action to be successful. The system I have developed will allow you to hunt in a good area every year. This system is a four year strategy for drawing in good trophy areas. It may not fit every hunter's individual needs, so feel free to modify it geographically to fit your own preferred style of hunting. It is essential to specialize in hunting a certain type of terrain. Whether it be the high mountain basins, rimrock-sagebrush country, or the cedar-oak brush desert of the southwest, stick to the terrain with which you are most comfortable.

First area: I always begin by attempting to attain a permit for Idaho.

1-2: Laverne's high mountain Wyoming mule deer has a true 30-inch main frame.

Remember, it's a first-come, first-served limited quota tag that can be obtained by simply calling the state of Idaho and using your credit card. Once an Idaho permit is obtained, I know if I fail to draw in any other state I will still have a backup hunting area. It is vital to have an area such as this in your back pocket. Why? Because the number one reason a trophy hunter becomes successful is that he becomes very good at hunting a particular terrain and geographic area. I personally specialize in hunting the high country and therefore will try to hunt this type of terrain throughout several western states.

Second area: The second area I try for would be one of Wyoming's top trophy producing areas. These are on a draw for nonresidents and you can only expect to draw a permit about every other year. When applying for these permits be sure to stick with the same area every year. This maximizes your ability to learn one area exclusively.

Third area: My third area will be one of the high mountain early hunts in Colorado or Utah. These states are on a preference point system and at the time of this writing it only takes one or two preference points to draw. With any luck, I should be able to draw one of these areas every couple of years. Again, it's important to find a good area and stick with it. Don't fall into the trap of jumping from area to area just because of a bad winter or down cycle in the deer population that year.

1-3: This huge TF Idaho deer is one of Laverne's best trophies.

Fourth area: I will apply for a couple of high profile trophy areas such as Arizona's Kaibab or Utah's Paunsaugunt and San Juan Elk Ridge. You never know, you could get lucky. You simply can't draw if you don't apply. However, to hinge your entire fall on the hopes of drawing one of these areas is the way you end up with nowhere to hunt.

This four-year plan was once again proven legitimate by Laverne Caldiera who called me a few years ago. He was frustrated because he hadn't been able to take a buck over 27 inches that would break into the 170-plus Boone and Crockett category. He had hunted the same area for the past 15 years looking for that 30-inch plus buck. From my experience, I knew this was a good area for a 140 to 150 type buck, however it wasn't what I would consider a prime trophy producing area. I suggested he research a few other regions in Wyoming.

He subscribed to *The Eastmans' Journal* and began running down leads on areas from the Potential Trophy Chart. He began using llamas and coyoting out in the high country (Fig. 1-1, pg. 16). The first year, he found and hunted a good area and was able to take a 30-inch buck in the 180 class (Fig. 1-2, pg. 18). Over the next four years, he collected several large deer throughout Idaho and Wyoming with the use of these very same techniques (Fig. 1-3, pg. 19).

This hunter took a little information and guidance and turned it into a collection of hard-to-acquire trophy mule deer. He did his homework and put in the time needed to collect some good trophies.

The only way to make this plan work relies on your ability to hunt the same area every year for the next four years. By doing this you are able to monitor deer behavior and buck movements within the area. Over time you will become more and more successful at locating trophy bucks in the area. I have found most successful trophy hunters have taken their three largest mule deer from the same type of area or creek drainage over an extended period of time. In fact, most of the trophies in their collection have come from the same type of terrain even though taken from different states.

With the plan outlined in this section and the determination to stick with it, you will begin seeing more trophy bucks and hopefully soon thereafter harvest a very nice buck for your collection. Your worst enemy isn't other hunters or areas without trophy mule deer, it's lack of patience with an area and the temptation to jump from hot spot to hot spot. Remember, consistency and proficiency are your allies. Hunting a given area consistently and becoming proficient at hunting that area will maximize your chances. While other hunters are crying the blues, you'll be in the know about good mule deer areas and have a better grip on trophy mule deer hunting. By putting together a plan starting today you'll be on track to becoming a more successful trophy mule deer hunter.

A friend, Bryon Wilson, and I took these nontypical bucks on the same day. It was 36 degrees below zero.

Chapter 2

Finding an Area

The first and most crucial step in the search for a trophy mule deer is locating a good area. So often I hear hunters complaining of too many other hunters in their area. On the other hand, I have found plenty of country that doesn't get hit hard. I look for areas with fewer forest service trails and country rough enough to discourage most other hunters. I would rather hunt in an area with fewer deer and fewer hunters than in a high profile area with too many hunters. There will always be rough areas with little traffic because most hunters won't exert the necessary physical effort it takes to hunt there. The majority of hunters elect to stay near established trails.

It is not easy to find these good areas. You will need to come up with a well-organized system for analyzing your information. The following steps will help you develop an information base for finding trophy areas.

Research

First you must find an area that has the potential to produce the type of trophy animal you are looking for. It is a waste of your valuable time and effort to hunt in an area where there are no bucks of the quality you seek. To do this most effectively, you will need several different sources from which to draw up-to-date information. Get a subscription to *The Eastmans' Journal* and other trophy hunting magazines such as the Foundation For North American Sheep, Bowhunter and Safari Club International. Journals such as these often supply very accurate up-to-date information on trophy producing areas throughout the western states.

Also be sure to acquire a copy of the latest harvest statistics published by the game departments in each of the western states. These publications contain crucial information such as herd counts, buck-to-doe ratios, preference points needed to draw and the number of hunters in the field. A good researcher would never draw a conclusion about an area without this type of information. This data is very cut and dried and serves as an excellent basis for eliminating areas of lesser quality.

Try to attend hunting shows where you can talk to other trophy hunters and outfitters. You need to create a networking system for gathering information that will help you make the best possible decisions regarding hunting areas. Get into the trophy hunting information loop! Phone calls are cheap, so keep in contact with agency personnel in the areas you are researching. Periodically dial up taxidermists you have found who consistently mount trophy class mule deer for clients. Throughout the West there is a contingency of taxidermists who are renowned for mounting trophy mule deer. These individuals may not tell you an exact area, but they often willingly lend information which creates a good starting point for your research. On the same line of thought, get acquainted with as many official Boone and Crockett scorers as possible. There are certain scorers out West who consistently measure a majority of the potential record book mule deer. Above all, keep in contact with other trophy mule deer hunters. Networking amongst fellow trophy hunters will often pay off tenfold.

Be sure to carefully document all of your gathered information and tips. Record everything you learn about an area including the hunt dates, times for scouting, and the portion of the season you will be hunting. You'll also need to know what type of weather conditions cause the animals to migrate out of a particular range or area. When hunting in the high country it becomes extremely important to know when the bucks leave. You can't kill a trophy that is not there. Lastly, write down your reasons for selecting or eliminating a certain area. You may need to refer back to this at a later date for justification's sake.

Look at, and compare the deer that have been taken from a certain area recently to your personal benchmark for a trophy. Too many trophy hunters simply look in the record book and think that's all it takes to find a trophy producing area. Many areas that have never produced a record book head hold good 180-class mule deer or possibly, big trash factor bucks that do not exceed the minimum scores to qualify for entry into the record book. When looking at a potential trophy area, the gross size of the racks for which it produces is of more interest than simply the total number of heads it has placed into the record book.

Each spring, you should make phone calls to inquire about herd conditions in your hunting area. Also look for any changes in the hunting proclamations for the next season. Collect articles and other bits of information pertaining to each area. Start a hit list of areas and begin narrowing it down until you come up with an area that is most conducive to your particular style of hunting and has the potential to produce the quality of head you are looking for.

Many hunters just want the quick fix...they want someone to tell them exactly where and when to hunt. Often an area that is productive for one hunter will not be quite right for another. Each individual must find the type of area that is best suited to his style of hunting. You will be much better off in the long run if you rely on your own research and evaluation when choosing an area.

Get Organized

Once you begin collecting information, you'll need to organize it in a way that makes it handy to locate. Keep a folder on each area and place every scrap of information on that area into the file. From these, you will eventually compile a worksheet for each potential area. I rate each area using a set of criteria such as...trophy potential, terrain, hunting pressure and accessibility. You should make up your own worksheets using your own personal set of criteria.

Develop A Plan Of Action

After choosing an area, it's time to write an in-depth plan of action. This includes a list of all major creek drainages, pockets and basins which you may want to investigate. Make sure to scout the area before the season if possible. This is a great way to eliminate unproductive portions of your area without losing crucial hunting time during the season. It serves as a great device for narrowing down the area you will be hunting.

Commitment

Once you have chosen an area, a total and complete commitment to your area will give you an extra edge. Hunt it for at least three or four years. Don't waver from your plan or get discouraged if you don't take a buck every year. Remember, you are looking for that buck that is one-in-500, and they don't grow on trees. He has five seasons under his belt and he's not dumb. When you continue to hunt the same area each year, you will eventually begin to understand where the mature bucks are during certain times of the year. This is the key which unlocks the secret to being successful in your area. It is much easier to hunt trophy bucks if you know were they will be during the hunt.

Keeping A Written Journal

Always carry a notebook with you into the field while scouting or hunting. This enables you to record vital information that may otherwise be forgotten after the season. Don't be fooled, you can't possibly retain all of this information in your head. A written journal is one of your best research tools. Information on weather conditions, deer behavior and access into a particular basin is invaluable to you for the next season. Get into the habit of writing down your scouting and hunting experiences at the end of each day. In the off season you can review it to help devise hunting and stalking strategies for the next hunting season.

When you keep a journal, don't overlook temperatures, weather conditions and any deer movements you observe. It will help you understand the habits of the bucks in the area, you will also begin to recognize possible trends that will help you score. I have a separate notebook for each area I hunt. All of the information compiled year after year on that particular area stays together in one file. That way, you have past years' information at your fingertips. Several days before I leave on my hunting trip I will set down and review my past notebook on that particular area. Then carry the notebook with me which allows me to refer back to information gathered in past years.

Being able to jot down information in the field is invaluable. I keep several journals, one on each area I hunt. During the off season, I store them in a file cabinet with the rest of the material for researching trophy areas.

This might sound like overkill, but it's not. The first year a hunting buddy went with me, he laughed at my ritual of writing everything down. By the next year, however, he was sold on it. All I had to do was go back into the journal for information about a particular escape route a buck had taken when leaving his high basin bedding area. By using that written down information, my buddy was able to take that buck who was now two years older and scored in the 180s.

Information gathered during the off season may also be recorded in your journal. When traveling, stop at taxidermy shops and sporting goods stores. You should ask questions about the quality of heads taken in different areas. This written information will not only give you a jump on other hunters, but your journal will be a history of your hunting adventures that can be enjoyed for all your life.

Obtaining Maps Of Your Area

Good topo maps are essential to your research effort. In some areas deer will travel up to 70 miles to their wintering ranges. These deer have to begin traveling in mid-October in order to make it over some of the high mountain passes before the snow gets too deep. In most cases, high mountain mulies won't stay at 10,000 feet when the October snows come. You can use your topo maps to estimate and plot their locations and movements throughout the fall.

Remember, some areas in the West will be void of game if the weather changes drastically. Ask biologists and game wardens about herd wintering areas and the general routes deer take to get there. If your area has a past history of early snows that move the game out, you need to know where they go and if it's still in your hunting area. Getting a permit for a good trophy area and then missing the deer due to the migration is a common occurrence.

You can order topographical maps from your local U.S.G.S. map outlet. However they sometimes have a problem finding your specific map numbers from the thousands available. The easiest approach is to call the United States Geological Survey, (U.S.G.S.) located in Denver, Colorado, and ask them to send you a set of map directories for every state that you plan to hunt. Each set consists of two parts, a catalog and an index. You'll need both to place an order.

The Index to Topographical Maps helps you locate the desired map. Once you know which region(s) you plan to hunt, you can use the Catalog to Topographical Maps to find the map's corresponding order number. You should first order your maps in the 30x60 minute quadrangle size. These are big enough to enable you to view a large area of the state. Then order your more detailed 7.5 minute map directly from U.S.G.S or your local outlet. Be forewarned, it can take as long as 12 weeks to get maps directly from the U.S.G.S

In conclusion, the secret to finding good areas is to utilize a number of research tools. However, your most valuable tool in locating a trophy area is to network with other trophy hunters who share a common interest and goal, the pursuit of trophy mule deer.

Chapter 3

Scouting

Pre-season scouting is a very effective way to locate trophy mule deer in your hunting area. When I operated my hunting camp in the early 70s, hunters would pay a premium to hunt trophy mule deer with me. Having paid this price, they expected to see big deer and have a knowledgeable guide. For that reason, I would personally guide the early hunts in September up to the first week in October.

Beginning August 1, I would spend a month slipping around checking the mule deer nests in my area. If I just wanted 150- or 160-class mule deer, scouting wasn't necessary. However my clients expected an above average trophy, therefore I had to seek out that one in a hundred type buck (Fig. 3-1, pg. 26). Living in this area all my life I intuitively knew where the bucks would be hanging out during the early season.

I could also rely on the previous season as an indicator of where the top quality bucks might be found. A mule deer buck has a habit of going back year after year to the same area, often returning to the same bedding spot. Of course due to winter mortality from weather and predators, not all the mature bucks would return to the high country. This made it extremely important to look the area over to see which bucks had matured into trophy class mule deer since the previous season.

One of my most valuable tools was the journal I packed in my pocket. I kept a record of all the places where I found nests or bedding and feeding areas of younger bucks. A couple of years later I would go back and find these younger bucks who had by then matured. A buck has a habit of returning to the same areas. Sometimes he will move one basin over but generally he's found in the same area each year. Key in on this and can keep track of these bucks as their antlers grow over the years. Many of the guys I know who have taken good bucks use this tactic religiously.

Two major mistakes are consistently made by hunters when scouting mule deer. First, they often go right into the buck's living area, intruding and contaminating his nest with human activity. Wandering through a buck's territory will alert him to your presence immediately. In my experience, a mature buck that is jumped from his bedding area several times will inevitably vanish. He will move to his secondary living area often staying there until the time comes to move down the mountain for the rut. The terrain of the secondary liv-

3-1: Finding that 190-plus mule deer takes time and luck.

ing area for most bucks is usually the most rugged area he can find.

It is wise to find special lookout points miles from a buck's nest. A concealed spot from where you can glass a lot of country is best. From this vantage point you will be able to monitor and document in your journal vital information such as: buck sightings, deer movements, terrain features, escape routes and bedding areas. I make it a habit to review these entries from my journal again before the season. Your chosen vantage point should allow you to observe without intrusion into the deer's comfort zone. By concentrating on the heads of creek drainages or large portions of mountain ranges you should easily be able to find where bucks tend to hold up. These include pockets, basins, snow slides on steep peaks, and high ribbon cliffs. Remember, you don't have to be up close and personal to determine if a buck is worth spending time with during the hunting season. A good spotting scope will allow you to determine this with the comfort of miles between you and the buck.

Whether it be hunting or scouting, I prefer not to move around much in the high country. Rather, I elect to spend several days on one lookout, (coyoting out) glassing over large portions of country for extended periods of time. If nothing surfaces, I move to a new area under the cover of the midday sun when chances of being detected by deer are much less.

The second crucial mistake occurs when a hunter scouts early in August, but doesn't return to hunt until the middle of October or later. He is scouting the bucks in their summer mode. By the middle of October most of the bucks have moved off the high mountain peaks down into the heavy timber. Here the bucks wait for the next 30 days in anticipation of the upcoming rut. They have fragmented from their bachelor groups and the older trophy bucks have now become loners. The hunter is left above the tree line scratching his head wondering where the bucks have gone.

Scouting The Reds

From August 1 through September 1, mule deer are in what I call their summer mode. Most bucks have developed their full rack size by this time and the antlers are beginning the process of hardening inside their soft velvet cover. I use the term "Scouting the Reds" to refer to finding bucks during this time of year (Fig. 3-2. pg 32). The reference to "red" comes about when the morning sun hits a buck this time of the year. The color is a bright red that is visible from miles away with a spotting scope or binoculars. The deer stick out like a sore thumb or morning beacon on the sunlit hillside. This is why a properly selected vantage point will bring the sun up at your back in the morning maximizing your ability to spot the bucks.

This is without a doubt the perfect time to scout for big bucks in the high country. By September 1, their color begins to change to a fall gray which makes them much harder to see against the slate and granite-covered terrain they call home. If you scout during the Reds, you will find the bucks together in bachelor groups. By scoping early in the morning, you will easily pick up every buck feeding in an entire drainage. Keep in mind these bucks will be in the velvet and their racks may appear 30 to 40 percent heavier. Their tines will also appear to be about 15 percent longer than without the velvet. The velvet hair sticks straight out catching the soft morning sun, giving the antler the illusion of increased length and circumference. This must be taken into account when judging the size of trophy bucks during this time of year (Fig. 3-2a, pg 29).

The Early Hunter Gets The Trophy

Most mule deer hunters live some distance from their hunting area and may have a tough time getting away to scout. What is the best method of scouting an area that may be hundreds of miles away? One of the strategies I use is to combine your scouting and hunting trips into one.

Most hunters show up one or two days before the season and hope to find a good mule deer in those short few days. A good alternative is to go into your area a week before the season to scout, and spend only a few quality days hunting. By combining your scouting and hunting trip, you make the most effective use of your time. More than once I have sat on a buck until opening morning and taken him at first light.

Another advantage this tactic offers is that your scouting information is only a few days old when the season opens. Remember, after the first two days of the season, bucks are often pushed around by hunting pressure. Many end up in their rugged secondary areas, where they will hide out for days at a time without even coming out to feed. These conditions make trophy hunting even more difficult.

If you do find a good old buck when scouting immediately prior to the season, the best approach is to sit on him until the opening morning of season. In many high mountain areas the most productive time to hunt is the first few days of season before the bucks are stirred up and displaced.

If I can't make the first few days of the hunt, I usually wait until the middle of the season. This strategy also has its benefits because you often have the entire area to yourself. With this decrease in hunting pressure, the deer are more apt to fall back into a routine of feeding in the morning and evening. However, mid-season hunting can have its drawbacks. The bucks may have been pushed into heavy cover or steep terrain where they will remain for extended periods of time, possibly even the remainder of the hunting season. This makes glassing and stalking much more difficult.

In summary, if you plan to hunt the opener of an early, high country area, it is best to do your scouting in August. If you are unable to scout in August the best tactic is to combine your scouting and hunting into one trip. However if you are going into the area after the first week of the hunting season, you will need to include timber strips, patches and stands below the high mountain basins in your glassing efforts.

Scouting after the Season

It is extremely important to gain knowledge of the migration routes of the mule deer to their winter ranges. For years I had the unique opportunity of keeping detailed records on some of the deer migration routes within my home state of Wyoming. Determining which mountain range these bucks migrated from and then observing them during the December rut on the winter range gave me a good idea of the trophy potential in a given area. Locating good bucks on the winter range gave me a starting point for the following year's scouting efforts. I could then concentrate my time and resources on a particular mountain range were I knew certain bucks would spend the summer and fall. These winter grounds can be found in every western state. Just like in the high country, you can find a buck coming back year after year to the same wintering area. This phenomenon is documented in the Eastman videos time and time again. We have over the years filmed the life spans of several big bucks on the Wyoming winter ranges.

Forty years ago when I first began watching deer on the winter range

3-2a: Velvet hair sticks straight out catching the soft morning sun making a buck's rack look bigger.

I was normally all alone except for the occasional rancher checking his cattle. Unfortunately over the last few years, observing deer on the winter range has become an increasingly popular pastime. It is being abused by people trying to get closer and closer for photos of these monster bucks. Poaching is also a problem on the winter range. Many good bucks have been illegally killed and their antlers sold for thousands of dollars. Due to all of this, the idea of watching deer on the winter range meets with wide disapproval by state Game and Fish agencies and some mule deer enthusiasts who wish to lock out everyone except themselves from this natural treasure.

Conclusion

Pre-season scouting has more than once led a trophy hunter to a trophy buck. You must however scout in a smart, efficient manner. By using the tactics and techniques outlined in this section you will greatly increase your ability to locate a big buck in the high country. Remember one thing…your time is more wisely spent scouting and finding a trophy mule deer than blindly wandering around a creek drainage hoping to stumble upon a trophy buck during the heat of the hunting season.

As I say in the four-year plan, the best way to learn a buck's habits is to hunt an area over and over again. However, I know this isn't always realistic.

Section II

TACTICS

Photo by Rod Hart

Tip: **3-2: When the morning sun hits these bucks, their body's light up, thus the name "in the reds". You can see a buck from many miles away when he is in this stage.**

Chapter 4

Coyoting Out

Imagine this scene. It is two days before deer season opens in the high country. Three riders and a string of pack horses pick their way along the rocky trail of a canyon, the clinking of the horses' metal shoes echoing against the granite walls. They reach a patch of timber on a small bench at the bottom of the basin where the riders tie up their horses and begin setting up camp. One unpacks while another begins chopping firewood. The third sets up the tents and builds a roaring fire.

With all the noise and activity of building a camp, if there is a super buck anywhere in the country he is not going to hang around. During the cover of night he will slip away to the safety of his alternative living area. This may be in the next creek drainage or an isolated pocket. He doesn't necessarily have to be in the same drainage to hear what's going on and leave the country. This scenario goes on every fall in the high country. It's no wonder so many hunters never see a decent buck.

Mule deer hunting has changed drastically over the past 35 years. During my younger years, I hunted in the high country where mule deer bucks never saw a human all summer. In those days when jumped from their bed, bucks would run only a short distance, then stand broadside looking at you. This behavior gave them a reputation of not being very smart. Keep in mind, in those days most of the high country was seldom touched by hunters. However, this is the 90s and with all the human traffic along the mountain trails, trophy mule deer no longer behave the way they did years ago. Now an old buck will slip out of his bed, leave the country and never look back. Chances are you will never see him leave.

In order for a deer to grow into a super buck, he has to survive at least seven years of hunting pressure. He will most likely find a hole or an isolated canyon where he can hide out for the duration of the hunting season. Most mature bucks have learned to live in small areas, becoming almost nocturnal. Their movements consist simply of going to water once every three days and feeding right around their bedding area. This low-profile lifestyle is a factor in keeping the smart buck undetected and alive from season to season.

To counteract this pattern a hunter has to slip into the buck's territory with very little impact on the country. You have to be able to observe

bucks from a distance. *Coyoting out* is a term I use that depicts a style of hunting. It's more than just a strategy, it's a way of living in the outdoors that causes minimal impact on the country and the game. It can be adapted to any terrain throughout the West. Even in the good old days, I used this technique successfully to hunt trophy high mountain mule deer. It also works very effectively during the archery season elk rut.

If you watch a pair of coyotes hunting in the high country they will do the same thing. Laying on a ridge under a scrub pine, they watch the surrounding area and wait patiently for the perfect opportunity. You to have to be like a coyote when looking for that super buck. Slip into a creek drainage or basin and find a patch of scrub timber where you can shade-up with a panoramic view of the country without having to move around much. It will require several scouting and hunting trips into the area to find just the right glassing spot.

A hideout like this will enable you to stay in mule deer country while remaining totally isolated and unnoticed by the bucks you are watching. This is where I set up a coyote camp using only a one-man tent and gas stove for cooking. Remember, a mule deer's strongest sense is his hearing; then comes his sense of smell. He will not tolerate a campfire or the rattling of metal cooking equipment in his backyard. That type of smell and noise will carry for miles alerting him to your presence almost immediately (Fig. 5-1 and Fig. 5-2, pg. 37).

From your coyote camp you can stay under cover while you patiently glass and wait. When you find a good buck it will take time to learn his habits and bedding areas. Mule deer are hard to pattern so you have to be able to observe their comings and goings. I record in my log any observed movements of the deer in the basin, plus any other information that will help me to evaluate the area at a later time. Make sure you glass until it is too dark to see. Remember, a big mule deer usually only comes out to feed at dusk during the early fall. Having your camp right where you're glassing is a slick hunting style. If you take time, glassing for several days you will eventually spot every buck within glassing range of your coyote camp.

Even in areas with excessive hunting pressure you are better off staying put and watching. This will enable you to locate some escape routes where a smart old buck can slip off to escape the average hunter. This style of hunting requires patience and is definitely not for the guy who has to jump bucks every day to satisfy his visual hunting needs.

When coyoting out on top at 10,000 feet, I get a kick out of watching the predictable behavior of other hunters. Just like clockwork, you can see them hurrying down country 20 minutes after the sun goes down. They seem determined to reach their nice comfortable camps or a main trail before dark. Meanwhile, I remain living in the deer's backyard, watching and waiting for a buck to come out at dark to feed. The next morning I'm still there glassing during that precious 20 minutes before the amber sun lights up the basin. Being off the beaten path in a small basin tucked away on the north side of a

Tip: **5-4: Using the tree branches to help break up your silhouette is one way to keep bucks' from seeing you. If you're well concealed, a buck will be more apt to feed out into the open and carry on with his daily routine.**

peak, you can often catch a trophy buck out of his nest feeding.

The only time I move around while I'm coyoting out is to slip to a different lookout to glass some new country. If possible, I always stay concealed in the scrub pines where I have my coyote camp set up right next to me. I never reveal myself by wandering around on the tops of the ridges with my silhouette against the skyline (Fig. 5-4, pg. 36). Mule deer have eight power eyesight and are accustomed to scanning the horizons and skylines for danger. Because ridges are the paths of least resistance, most hunters move along them like highways. Bucks have learned to bed down where they can scan many ridges at once for hunter traffic. To stay undetected you need to carefully plot your movements to minimize exposure. This is always a consideration when moving to a new area to set up a coyote camp. I learned this important lesson the hard way.

It was September 10, opening day of mule deer season. I tied my horses in a patch of timber on the backside of a ridge 400 yards from the top. On the opposite side was a large basin. I quietly slipped over the top and tucked myself under the branches of a drooping scrub pine just below the ridge line. The tree broke my outline and offered good shade, making it impossible for a buck to detect my presence. A large overhanging

Note: **5-1: Concealing my camp in pines helps to insure I remain hidden (see arrow). 5-2: Using a lightweight fly and not building a fire is important. This lightweight fly and camp is designed for hunting above timberline.**

branch was at just the right height for mounting my spotting scope attachment. I started to glass the basin carefully.

My first pass revealed four small bucks feeding on a bench on the opposite side of the basin. With the season only a few hours old and no shots being fired, the bucks were still in their summer feeding mode staying in the open until late morning. Above them on a steep slope was a good, heavy-horned 170 typical with a 27-inch spread. The buck was busy stripping his velvet on a weathered four-foot jack pine. He was really getting after it! It took him a short 10 minutes to totally strip his antlers of any velvet and turn them to a bright bloody red. I can still picture those antlers shining in the early morning sun.

After watching him for a while, I began glassing a nearby knife ridge that ran down from a peak to the floor of the basin below. Straight across the basin I spotted a lone buck lying under a scrub pine. The buck was warming himself in the early morning sun. He had 26-inch main beams with a 24-inch inside spread. The G-4 was at least 14 inches long. The back tines were 16 inches long and the G-3 branched low off the G-2. A four-inch cheater coming off the back tine gave him a 32-inch outside spread. He was a 190-plus super buck who didn't have a

Tip: **5-5: Skylining yourself like this will make your presence known to every buck in the basin. Never skyline yourself on open ridges or slopes!**

clue I was watching the basin even though his bedded position gave him the opportunity to watch any movement that occurred below him.

Suddenly the sky opened up and sheets of rain, thunder and lightning filled the basin. I grabbed my rifle and spotting scope and slipped back up over the ridge to where my horse was tied. After putting on my yellow slicker, I sat down under a clump of short trees to wait out the electrical storm. At this time of year the weather patterns develop these thunder bursts that just roll through leaving sunny skies soon afterward.

I'll have to say there is little in the outdoors that scares me; not snow storms, cold weather, bronky horses or even grizzly bears. However, one thing terrifies me…an electrical storm. I'm deathly afraid of them, especially in the high country. It also doesn't help to be on a horse that has metal shoes on. For some reason lightning has always gravitated toward me. Once a bolt struck not 200 yards away. It was so close that every hair on my body stood on end. These storms are most severe in late summer and early fall. Consequently, when it begins to lightning I get down off the high peaks in a hurry!

Luckily the storm blew over in 45 minutes and the sun came out to warm things up once again. Not thinking, I walked back to the top of the ridge to see if the big buck was still under that scrub pine. When I put

Chris
Lacey
1997
©

my glasses up, we met eyeball-to-eyeball. Even though I was over a 1/2 mile away, I was skylined wearing my yellow slicker. The old buck pegged me instantly. He slowly got up and climbed to the top of the peak. Just before he disappeared over the edge he stopped and glared at me one last time. As he stood skylined at 10,500 feet, his impressive rack reaching for nothing but blue Wyoming sky I said to myself, "I will find you this fall."

You know I looked in every basin in that drainage but never saw him again. He just vanished. As with many of those big high mountain bucks, the country just swallowed him up.

Having a super buck get away because of sloppy hunting habits is a hard lesson to learn for anybody (Fig. 5-5, pg. 39). Now, I am very careful about skylining myself because it's almost always a dead giveaway.

Remember, when you hunt a mule deer in the high country you are on his home range. Bucks seem to have a sixth sense that lets them know when their territory is being invaded by a human. We are the same way in our home, it doesn't take long for us to sense if someone else is there. A mature buck picks up on any unusual activity or noise, slipping off to his alternative living area in an instant.

It takes time to learn an area well enough to know where to put your coyote camp. However after a few trips into the country, it will become quite apparent. Two things necessary for finding bucks are discipline and commitment even when faced with adverse conditions.

Short Coyoting Trips

In the country where I was raised you can still find prime high mountain mule deer areas within a day's walk. Peaks and bowls that offer great trophy mule deer hunting are not far from many main roads and trail heads. These areas have produced some great mule deer hunting for me in the past. The way to hunt many of these areas is to go light for only a two-day pack in hunt taking just enough food to get by. I only hunt this way for the first two weeks of September after watching the weather reports beforehand to make sure it is going to be clear. I take only a wool blanket, leaving the 3.5-pound sleeping bag home. You'll find me spending a night in a patch of timber next to a snow slide or basin then as morning comes, I often catch groups of bachelor bucks out feeding.

This is a way to coyote out for a couple of days without having to take a large pack overloaded with a lot of gear. I designed a pack with an internal frame that can be used for day hunting or for one of these short coyoting trips (Fig. 5-6 and Fig 5-6a, pg. 42). It is made of Cordura and wool which makes it quiet, durable and functional. Throughout the West there exist many areas conducive to this type of hunting. In fact, in Colorado I have pulled off the interstate and taken off for a two-day coyoting out trip into country thousands of hunters have simply zipped by at 70 miles per hour. Finding these areas takes a little research but I assure you the West is full of them.

Remember, coyoting out is a way of living in the outdoors that does not impact the country or game. The strategy can be used for elk, deer

Note: **5-6: I use a one-man tent or lightweight fly. In my medium size wool internal-frame pack I carry a gas stove, lightweight sleeping bag, one medium stainless steel cooking pot and one change of socks. Going superlight for two days is an effective way to hunt deer. A fly is all that's necessary if hunting in good weather. Remember to watch the weather patterns on these trips... going light is great but not if it's going to rain or snow.**

Note: **5-6a: I have had this pack for 20 years. Its made out of cordura-wool so it's quiet and strong. The bottom is leather and I designed it to be able to take one or two day trips. The side pockets are for spotting scope and water bottles. Notice the elastic hooks to hold on sleeping bag and small fly tent. Also I use the Leupold 25x50 spotting scope, it's small and lightweight. In the high country weight is everything.**

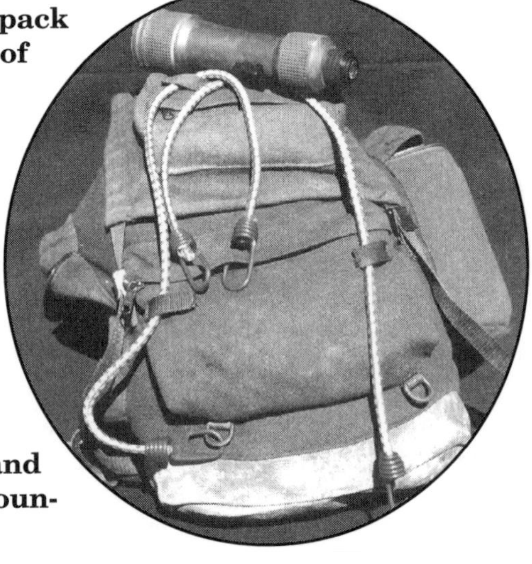

and sheep hunting anywhere in the West. It's a tough way of hunting but will produce for the guy who is willing to sacrifice comfort in the field for a quality trophy mule deer.

Bushwhacking

With the added hunting pressure over the years, super bucks have found even more isolated high country pockets to hide in. These areas consist of rocky peaks, steep snow slides and rugged cut out basins with no Forest Service trails. Here, there is little or no human activity. To reach these mule deer pockets you'll have to leave the beaten path and head across rugged country. I call this type of traveling "bushwhacking." (Fig 5-7a, pg. 44)

When you move from one hideout to another you'll sometimes have to hike along narrow game trails from peak to peak, or travel through country having no trails. This is where being able to find the easiest route through the rugged terrain becomes a real art. Unfortunately, it can only be learned through experience and practice.

Traveling in this country without the benefit of a well-maintained trail allows you to access country that is rarely hunted. The normal hunter takes the route of least resistance, traveling up established trails to the heads of creek drainages and hunting the most accessible country. He then follows the trail over the top into another drainage and hunts it in the same fashion. This leaves the rugged holes and pockets to the trophy bucks and the savvy hunter. To get into these areas you must be able to use deer trails and know how to traverse mountain faces. If you go into those isolated pockets on the back side of a peak you will find mule deer bucks.

One method I use to find access into the roughest country is checking for deer trails after a skiff of fresh snow has fallen. They will show up giving you an idea of how to move from one peak to another. Trails that go across rock slides or across a steep sidehill and through a saddle into another drainage are especially noticeable. I may not use these faint trails to hunt from, but you can bet I note their location in my journal for future use.

Looking for a way through timber can also be a challenge. More than once have I ended up in a real noisy mess waist deep in deadfall. One thing to remember is to look for large fir tree stands that are good indicators of a more open access across a mountain. Because of larger trees the chances of deadfall is less likely. Firs have less of a chance of falling over than do shallow-rooted lodgepole pines. Most of the time in these fir stands you will find game trails that work their way up. I always sketch in my journal a route into a new country. I do this because when I get over to the mountain it looks different and it can be difficult to remember the route you have plotted. Also if I come back the following year, I want to be able to have the location of the route at my fingertips. (Fig. 5-7, pg. 45) Because I didn't write it down, there have been several times when I have had to sit for hours trying to remember a route from the previous year into a small basin. Finding yourself wander-

Tip: **5-7b: High basins hold bucks especially if no main trails go through the country. For that reason, this particular area has very little human traffic and holds bucks early in the season.**

Tip: **5-7a: Most of this country has no maintained forest service trails and very little hunting pressure in the high pockets and slides in 1 and 2,**

Note: **5-7: I have hunted this area for 30 years and never seen another hunter. The only way into it is by using deer trails. Once in the basin, a good knowledge of the game trails is necessary to move from one area to another (I have them marked in my journal). 1.) I have found several bucks that call this high ridge home. Noting their age and bedding nest I can come back in several years to find them still hanging out in the same basin. That's providing a predator, hunter or winter kill hasn't claimed them. 2.) Traveling to this isolated pocket means going around that peak through the lower timber. It took several trips into the pocket to learn the location of the trails and the easiest way in. This is a pocket where bucks never see a hunter. It's just too isolated and rugged.**

ing around and possibly alerting a buck to your coming isn't worth it.

Another good way to find routes through the country is to study the deer movements. They will show you passages over and around mountains that aren't noticeable to the naked eye.

Over 50 years of activity in the back-country, Forest Service freeways have conditioned many trophy deer to live in holes away from high traffic trails. A buck will position his bed where he can watch all possible trails and routes into, through, and out of his world. Generally he has an escape route, a back door he uses to slip away to a secondary living area when pressured by human activity. Because of his ability to leave undetected, hunters generally don't have a clue the old buck was ever there.

Tip: **5-8b: Wool pants and top with lightweight polypro underwear were a good combination on this hunt. Using wool is great, if you get into bad weather it will save your life. I use only wool on these high country hunts.**

I only use Forest Service trails to access the high country. From there, all of my traveling is done by bushwhacking into pockets...pockets where access is not available through the use of maintained trails. My brother, Rod, and I made a video titled Mule Deer Action. In the film I take a good 30-inch buck. The country we hunted is off the main trail and throughout the years of hunting this area I have never seen another hunter. Believe it or not this pocket is in a general Wyoming hunting region. Remember, no trails...no hunters, no hunters...big mule deer.

I travel from one area to another along trails used only by mule deer. It's a good idea to check out the north sides of the peaks in your area. Not only do bucks live there, but it may also give you a different angle from which to glass. Rough areas like this are not accessible to the average trail walking hunter. To do this you must have a working knowledge of the area so you know where you're going. Topo maps can help, but there's no substitute for simply spending time in the country.

Usually, I study the game trails in an area through my binoculars to figure out a route to a good lookout. From there I can set up for a couple of days of coyoting out. Using this technique enables you to locate trophy bucks that have moved into these remote areas to escape the hunting pressure from the leisurely trail hunter.

Tip: **5-8: I am on top of a pass just heading into another drainage to hunt. Back in the early 80s we made a habit of packing only 40 pounds. Taking only the necessities and using food caches allowed us to extend our hunting range.**

Backpacking

Thirty-five years ago when I started hunting mule deer, most people were typically hunting the late seasons down on the winter ranges. I personally preferred to backpack into the high country early in September. Back then backpacking allowed me to be extremely mobile in this rough country. The equipment was very limited and the dried food of the day was barely eatable. My white gas stove was temperamental, but it allowed me to cook without building a fire. The single man tent was a heavy version designed for mountain climbing. Backpacks were made with heavy frames with no hip belts or padded shoulder straps (Fig 5-8, pg. 47). Consequently, the weight of the pack would pull on your shoulders and back making a day of traveling the high country extremely miserable.

Back then, I would take a seven-day trip once a year in early September. After that I would take short two-day trips whenever I could throughout the remainder of the fall. It wasn't uncommon to make one of these seven-day trips without seeing another person. At that time, most people preferred to hunt elk, but since the area I hunted had very few elk, hunters didn't waste their time there.

By the early 80s equipment had changed drastically. The packs were designed with padded hip belts to help transfer some of the weight from your shoulders. We no longer had to eat dried food. Instead, there were full dinners that could be thrown into boiling water and heated in minutes. Stoves became very reliable and the equipment was finally designed with weight in mind.

Every outdoor writer will give his personal, mile-long list of things to carry in your pack. Keep in mind, most of these guys aren't hard-core. They normally hike on well-maintained Forest Service trails rather than bushwhacking through rough country where water is non-existent and weight is of crucial concern. Half of their gear list is designed to make you more comfortable. This just isn't practical for excessive physical exertion over 10,000-foot peaks and across steep rocky slides or basins.

When it comes to choosing the gear you need, you are the only one who can determine your own personal comfort level...which often outweighs your ability to carry it. If this tends to be the case, you may be better off considering a llama, goat or mule. I don't intend to tell you what to pack into the high country, rather I'll give you a few suggestions you may find helpful.

Clothing is the most important factor in determining exactly what conditions you can comfortably endure. Layering with wool and polypropylene underwear is a great way to deal with the changing weather patterns you will come across at high elevations. I use a down or a wool coat combined with a wool shirt for extreme weather. I prefer wool because when it gets wet, it still has outstanding insulating value. My pants are lightweight wool with a diamond-shaped wedge sewn into the crotch for extra freedom of movement when walking and climbing in rugged country. I carry three pairs of socks that I hand-wash when soiled. A lightweight GoreTex raincoat with a hood, warm cotton gloves and a wool hunting hat takes care of my clothing needs.

The need for wool pants was driven home one fall when my partner and I backpacked into a basin for several days to hunt bucks. It was September 9,

5-12: I photographed Carl as he was packing out one of the trophy bucks we took on a backpack trip. With the meat, we were packing 110-pound plus packs out of that 10,000-foot country.

Note: **5-9: The most reliable lightweight stove I've found is the Whisper Lite. It runs on white gas and doesn't take long to heat up a dinner or soup.**

Note: **5-9a In the high country, weather can change from summer to winter in a matter of minutes. Because of its insulating factor even when wet, wool is the only type of clothing I will take with me when I coyote out. Notice the pen light with the clip on my hat. I use it when cooking after dark.**

Note: **5-9b I carry matches, toilet paper, butane lighter, a flint striker and some type of fire starter sticks all in a heavy-duty plastic ziplock bag. I also carry one good knife and ceramic sharpening sticks. I carry a small flashlight and two self-heating hand warmers. The binoculars are Leupold 10x35s and the spotting scope is a lightweight Leupold 25x50 fixed power. Everything is geared toward being light just for coyoting out.**

and had been raining for two days nonstop. After watching the weather report, it looked as if it would clear off the next day as high pressure made its way in from the west coast. Well, my partner had good old denim pants. All day we bushwhacked through high mountain grass and vegetation as it poured rain and spit snow. He stayed wet and cold from his waist down while I was warm and comfortable in my light wool pants. By the time we got to our destination he had the initial signs of hypothermia.

The next day after the weather cleared off, he remained wet all day until the vegetation dried out. Denim or cotton isn't much good if the weather turns bad and the material gets wet.

For cooking, I pack one stainless steel pot, cup, spoon and a small coffee can to boil water for soup or coffee (Fig. 5-9, pg. 50 and Fig 5-10 pg. 52). You'll need to stay as clean as possible…a small bar of soap and wash cloth takes care of me quite well. I also pack a small bag containing powdered soap for washing dishes and my sweaty socks. It doesn't take long for a pair of socks to get salty from perspiration and start rubbing your feet raw.

When it comes to food, I use pre-made dinners that you just boil in water because no dishes are required. After a hard day of hunting just drop them

Tip: **5-10: One of our coyoting out spots with a lookout from which we can watch a lot of country. I like to use a lean-to because of its light weight. If used properly it will keep the weather off, but remember to put the back of your lean-to toward the weather. If the weather gets too bad I will pull the front down lower. In a major storm I will move down to lower country and wait.**

into boiling water and they're ready to eat. These dinners contain fat which conventional freeze-dried food lacks. You need to burn fat for energy during long days of climbing. I also throw in some powder drink mix for a beverage. For lunches, rolls and sliced meat pre-packaged in daily portions are ideal. A large block of cheese and several cups of Ramen noodles also serve as a good warm lunch alternative. For breakfast I pack instant oatmeal, Hostess pies and coffee. Candy, power bars and small cans of fruit top off my high country grocery list. I package each meal in its own plastic sealed bag. It's not much of a gourmet delight but it's good enough to get me through the hunt.

Though backpacking is one of the most effective ways to hunt high mountain deer, it does have its share of drawbacks. The biggest problem can be the increased weight of packing out a trophy mule deer. In the early 80s I would go with a hunting partner. The two of us could de-bone a buck and pack out the meat, cape and horns in one trip. This would only allow for one deer to be taken during the trip. More than once we would stash our food in a tree to give us more room in our packs for the meat and antlers. It wasn't uncommon to lug 110-pound packs out to the trailhead.

I'm convinced those years of trekking with heavy packs caused cartilage damage to my knees in addition to arthritis and bone spurs in my joints.

Note: **5-10b: I secure my rifle to the back of the pack in a heavy soft gun case. It travels a lot nicer than trying to keep it on my shoulder along with my heavy backpack straps. I have never jumped a big buck going from one area to the next. So having my rifle on the ready was just a wishful attempt at jumping one up. I also use the elastic hooks to tie on anything else that I want to bring out. My pack's top frame can extend 6 inches for tying on antlers (see arrow). With everything, my pack weighs 38-41 pounds plus rifle.**

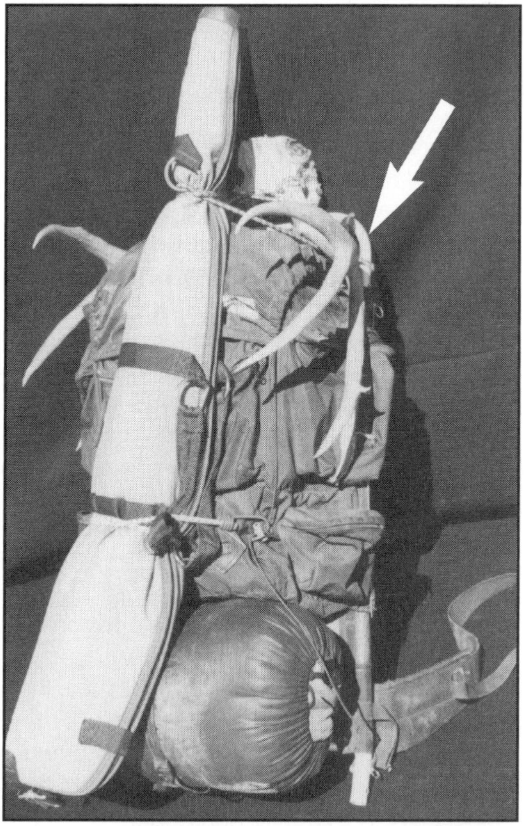

Note: **5-11: These days you must take a two-stage water purifier to filter out Giardia and other parasites in the water. Don't go into the back country without one or you may regret it in the near future...21 days to be exact, the gestation period for Giardia. If you find yourself on a high peak with only a trickle of water, you can screen out the bad particles and keep from having to hike down to the creek below.**

However, being young we healed fast and just kept pressing on. Unfortunately, between horses and backpacking the high country it has caught up with me and now my knees are just about worn out.

For the first few years, we couldn't keep our packs under 45 pounds and carry enough food for a full ten-day trip. It got to be a game to see how light we could go into the high country. My hunting partner, Carl Oksanen (Fig. 5-10a, pg. 55) usually went extremely light. He would take only a nylon tarp for cover, eliminating the weight of a one-man tent. If it rained or snowed, he would just wrap his sleeping bag up in it. Otherwise, he threw it down as a ground tarp underneath his sleeping bag. I bought one of the first GoreTex prototype sleeping bag shells. It worked very well in bad weather and weighed only 29 ounces making it a great alternative to a heavy seven-pound tent. We both had lightweight 3/4 body length foam pads. Including food, our packs were only in the 45-pound range.

I always hated to shoulder my rifle while backpacking into our coyoting spots. With the backpack straps on your shoulders, your rifle sling continually slips from your shoulder. This made it extremely uncomfortable to pack a rifle for an extended period of time. The added seven pounds of my rifle on one side constantly made me feel off balance. You know there wasn't a single time I jumped a monster buck on my way from one coyoting spot to another. For this reason I began to carry my gun on the back of my pack (Fig 5-10b, pg 53). I bought a good quality soft cover gun case and used bungee cords to secure it. It works real slick and when we got to the hunting area out came the rifle in a matter of seconds. Throughout years of strapping the gun to my pack I never once had the scope or gun damaged.

Because of our excessively light gear, if a storm rolled in we would move down 1,500 feet into the creek bottom and build a comfortable camp complete with a fire and tarp lean-to. There we would hold up until the weather broke, even if it took several days. After it cleared we were back on the high ridges and peaks coyoting out in our same spots; glassing, looking and waiting for Mr. Big.

In our quest for ever lighter packs, we often didn't take enough food and would have to hike to the trailhead in the middle of the hunt for more. Unfortunately when this happened we burned up two precious hunting days. This inability to carry enough food made it impossible to get back to some of the more remote mule deer country.

In an effort to cure the problem, I began building food caches at various campsites during my pre-season scouting in late August. Suddenly our range of operation had been extended. Now we were able to get into those more remote areas that were previously so hard to reach because of food, water and weight restrictions. Our packs were lighter and we were able to cover country faster and reach our destination in better physical shape.

Unfortunately, back in my backpacking days I caught Giardia. At the time we knew little about this parasite and consequently overlooked its symptoms. I went four years before being diagnosed, in fact last fall I got it a second time. Thank goodness for those pills! (Fig. 5-11, pg. 53) Now you can pack a two-stage water purifier that will filter any junk or parasites from even the smallest stream coming from the side of a peak. I highly recommend you

5-10a: My mule deer hunting and backpacking buddy, Carl Oksanen, with his good luck Budweiser mug hanging off his pack, (never go to the hills without it).

make this a permanent item in your pack throughout your travels in the West.

Packing enough water was another problem. Most of our campsites were well above most water sources. Caching water at the campsites during August scouting trips proved even more important than food. I used a simple burlap grain sack packed with two gallons of water and some canned goods. I would hang it high in a tree on a secluded ridge away from the beaten path.

It is important to put the food in airtight containers inside the burlap bag. The heavy-duty plastic containers will withstand mice and squirrels but they are no match for the teeth of black or grizzly bears. For that reason we climbed high up the tree and hung the bag from a large branch with a rope. It needs to be far enough off the ground so no bear can get to it. At times I would also place a canister of gas for the stove in one of the caches. We always looked forward to the next cache as our food and water would usually be exhausted by the time we arrived.

I think backpacking is still the best way of finding a big buck. It is definitely the most mobile and eliminates the excess burden of having to take care of pack animals, leaving you to spend 100 percent of the time looking for a good buck (Fig. 5-12, pg. 49).

Tip: **5-14a: The timber strips along a basin's wall are ideal areas to find a mule deer nest. When glassing make sure to look these places over carefully.**

Llamas

Llamas can be an excellent alternative to using horses or even backpacking. They can go anywhere you can walk which gives you the flexibility of camping on the high rocky ridges where there are no trails. When it gets dark you can just throw your sleeping bag down on the ground and call it camp.

I have found llamas to be more user friendly than horses. If their pack slips they will just lie down and wait for you to re-pack it. Because they are a part of the camel family, llamas can go three days without water. That is a real advantage when you are coyoting out on a 10,000-foot peak where water is 1/2 mile away straight down. Also, they have soft padded feet that make little or no noise while traveling across a rock slide. A good llama is able to pack 60 pounds, making them my top choice when hunting this type of country.

The year we filmed Mule Deer Action, we used llamas to hunt the high country of Wyoming. It was filmed in a basin with no horse trails

5-13: While filming the video Mule Deer Action with my brother, Rod, we packed camera gear and hunting equipment into remote areas looking for big bucks.

5-14b: A 28-inch buck I took off the mountain in the background. Our llamas sure came in handy for packing the deer off that rugged peak.

where if you took a buck, you packed it out on your back (Fig. 5-13, pg. 57). After I shot the 30-inch buck in the video, we walked those llamas right into the bottom of the basin, loaded the deer on two of them and climbed straight up a vertical slide and out over the top. Since then I have been sold on llamas as pack animals in rough mule deer country.

One disadvantage of llamas is you can walk them into the ground if you are in good physical condition. Be careful, take it slow and the llamas will easily last the entire trip (Fig. 5-14, pg. 59). Besides, if you go slow you will get to know the country better and find areas you might otherwise have overlooked. Llamas are also subject to hypothermia if exposed to wet snow for a prolonged period of time. If this happens, you need to get them into a covered area where they can dry their wool. Their wool may be heavy, but if they get wet and cold down to their skin, it can mean real trouble.

If you pack light, two llamas per person seems to be a good rule of thumb. Some hunters may choose to take several pieces of luxury equipment, therefore using more llamas becomes essential. Although this provides for a comfortable camp, having a large string of llamas makes it easier for a trophy buck to be aware of your presence in his territory.

5-14: Here I adjust a pack on one of the llamas. We take two animals per hunter leaving only the rifles and a daypack to be carried by the hunter.

There are several great books published on the subject of llamaneering in the high country. Many hunters like to use llamas for only a few weeks in the fall, but they don't want to board them year around. That's where a guy like Wes Holmquist in Pocatello, Idaho (208-232-9016) comes in. He will rent you llamas for a very reasonable rate. He also allows you to reserve the same set year after year. For first-time users, Wes offers a one-day school where you can learn the ins and outs of handling and packing llamas. If you decide you would like to own one, he sells good mountain-wise llamas, fully trained.

5-14c: John Capel works his way up a steep face with one of his pack goats.

5-14d: Famed goat packer, John Capel, on a successful high mountain mule deer hunt.

Pack Goats

Pack goats are another fine alternative that will enable you to get into the rugged terrain of the trophy mule deer. Goats also allow you to live with the game for days at a time without returning to the trailhead.

Adult billies can carry up to 50 pounds, but nannies also make fine packers and can carry 30 to 40 pounds. Goats thrive on any available vegetation, a quality unique to goats' super-efficient digestive systems. Goats, like llamas, can go three days without water if the vegetation has good moisture content. Many mule deer hunters now use goats to coyote out and have found them to be extremely effective. Using two goats per hunter is a good rule of thumb. Like llamas, goats enable you to lug more equipment into the hills.

John Capel of Rocky Mountain Pack Goats is the front runner in innovative pack gear design, manufacturing, breeding, training and sale of proven pack goat stock. He also has a referral service for pack goats that involves qualified breeders in several western states. If you would like to learn more about John's pack goats, send inquires to Rocky Mountain Pack Goats, 1241 S. First Ave., Thatcher, Arizona 85552.

5-15a : Mike Eastman in the early 70s guiding trophy mule deer hunters above timberline in Jackson Hole, Wyoming.

Horse Hunting in the High Country

When it comes to using saddle horses as a tool for high mountain mule deer hunting in the 90s, they are a definite disadvantage. At 10,000 feet, there isn't much in the way of good horse feed and it's often a 2,000-foot descent to the creek bottom for water. It's a waste of time to climb for two hours every day to get back onto the ridges where the deer live. Horses need to be watered daily, and at these elevations the only water is that which you carry.

Another disadvantage is that horses are noisy. Their iron shoes can be heard for miles as they walk along the rocky trails. They also have a habit of blowing, snorting and whinnying which will certainly alert attentive mule deer.

There are limits to where you can take a horse. There are just not enough passable horse trails among the rock slides. Horses can, however, be used to get you to the lower reaches where you can set up a spike camp to use as a jumping off point for the high basins.

Over the years my style of hunting has changed. In the 60s and 70s, I could use horses to get into the high country because the only human traffic was the domestic sheepherders. They would push their flocks from basin to basin grazing on the alpine grass. They were never a threat to the deer. A big buck would stay in a basin or snow slide even if it had sheep trails winding through it.

In the 80s, hunting this thin-air country became more popular. The majority of those hunters used horses to get around, but they were only able to hunt a relatively short distance from their mounts. With more and more traffic, these areas began to produce fewer and fewer mature deer and more and more smaller, immature bucks. I went back to back-

5-16: Back in the 70s I had to use horses to get the hunters up into this high country. This is one of the few photos taken of me over many years of guiding. Back then most of my area hadn't been hunted and the bucks weren't as elusive as they are today.

5-17: Here I am looking over some of the vast country in my outfitting area, notice how steep it is. I was able to build horse trails into most of this country which allowed me to guide hunters in some of the best trophy mule deer country in Wyoming.

packing and hunting the more rugged areas.

Don't get me wrong, you can use a pack horse to slip into an area and hunt bucks just be more aware of your impact on the country. Horses do make more noise and require more water and feed.

These days trophy hunters have to be able to move quickly with as little impact on the terrain as possible. The key is keeping your equipment simple and lightweight. Only the bare necessities are packed, leaving the bulky luxury items at home. Catching a buck out of his hideout without him knowing you are there is the hunting strategy of the future.

5-15: I still use horses on some hunts but only to get into the general area, or in this case to pack out a couple of bucks.

Tip: **4-2: Having a large area to glass is one of the keys to finding bucks. The area beyond me doesn't have a Forest Service trail into it. In the 35 years I have hunted it, never have I seen another hunter.**

Chapter 5

Glassing

There are numerous articles out there recommending what type of optical equipment to use and how to glass for big bucks. The standard theory is to carry big, heavy 18x50 binoculars so you can watch a deer wiggle his ear in the heavy brush two miles away. However, when you're hunting at 10 to 11,000 feet packing everything on a llama or your back, weight is crucial. Personally, I feel these huge binoculars are nice but not necessary for finding high mountain bucks.

In my experience, a pair of 10x40s with the auto-focus feature are ideal for high country hunting. They are lightweight and crystal clear. Use whatever works best for you, but for the cost you can't beat Leupold. Ten years ago, I made a sling and pocket that helped disperse the weight of the binoculars onto my chest and shoulders. It was much better than having all the weight hanging on my neck all day. If it would snow or rain the binoculars were protected and kept dry in this pocket. Now you can get a similar product from Crooked Horn Outfitters (805-822-3635) called the "Bino-System."

For locating game at great distances in the high country, my spotting scope is more valuable than binoculars. There are many good scopes on the market, but I prefer a 25x Leupold with a 50mm objective lens. It weighs almost nothing and has great light gathering capabilities for evening glassing. Its compact size and shape fit perfectly into the side pocket of my coyoting pack. My experience with variable power spotting scopes has been frustrating. When you crank them up to 30 or 40 power, the heat waves can cause major distortion and their light gathering ability is poor. This can cause frustration when trying to size up a trophy buck in poor light. They can also add more weight to your pack than a fixed power.

Most complaints about using a spotting scope center on eye fatigue. Looking with one eye while squinting the other can make your eyes hurt. Keeping both eyes open while looking through your spotting scope will drastically reduce eye fatigue. I learned this trick years ago after many hours of squinting through my spotting scope. Keep both eyes open, concentrate and focus looking through the scope with your master eye (the eye you shoot with). At first, both eyes want to focus together but suddenly, you will be able to focus clearly through the scope with the one eye while the other remains open. You may have trouble keeping

4-1: This spotting scope holder has many advantages over the conventional tripod.

both eyes open for long periods of time so try alternating between keeping one eye open and both eyes open. Using this technique, I can spend many hours looking through a spotting scope. This method of glassing takes time to learn, but with patience it can be mastered by most hunters. It will enable you to spend more time behind the spotting scope while improving your chances of spotting that trophy buck.

Hand holding a spotting scope in a steady position is almost impossible. In some cases you may want to pack a small tripod, but there again the weight and bulkiness of a tripod are a definite consideration. Personally, I prefer the freedom of being able to grab my scope and start glassing immediately without having to set up a tripod. I use anything that becomes handy for a support...rocks, a hat or even my pack.

A good alternative to a tripod is using a simple lightweight spotting scope attachment that can be screwed into a scrub pine tree trunk or large branch. This device provides a steady rest yet allows you to swivel the scope around as well as up and down. It works especially well while coyoting out, as you will usually be camped in a clump of trees. The weight of this attachment is mere ounces. A commercial version is

Tip: **4-3: When glassing against the grain of the terrain, there is much of the country you won't be able to see.**

available from Swarovski, or you can build your own from a screwdriver (Fig 4-1, pg. 68).

Glassing With The Grain Of The Terrain

The high country is made up of creek drainages which usually have their beginnings in a snow bank or a high basin spring. From there, they run down into another creek and eventually into a river. When you come into the head of one of these drainages, you need to spend most of your time glassing high pockets, slides and knife ridges that run up to the peaks. A pocket is a thin clearing between two strips of timber. It could be a small opening no bigger than a vehicle, or perhaps a snow slide with a green patch of lush grass at the top. Any little place like this is where you may find a big mule deer's nest. He will only slip out to feed at dusk and dawn right around that small clump of cover. To locate a big buck in an area like this you have to learn how to glass with "the grain of the terrain."

If you study a person who is very familiar with hunting a certain area, you'll notice he always goes to one particular spot from where he

Note: **4-4: Moving farther in one direction you find that more of the mountain opens up for you to glass. You are glassing with the gain of the terrain. 1.) Bucks will live in the strips of timber and then move out to feed in the snow slides. 2.) Ribbon cliffs offer the buck cover and a perch to watch the whole creek drainage.**

can glass a large section of the country (Fig. 4-2, pg. 66). To the layman, the individual has found a high lookout where he can look over a lot of country. Actually, there is much more to the perfect glassing spot than finding the highest point in the area. Sure, you can glass a lot of country from that high vantage point, but can you glass it effectively? There may be areas that you just can't get a good look at such as a slide that is partially obscured by the tree line. You just can't see clearly those little spots that tend to hold bucks. If these problems sound familiar, you may be glassing against the grain of the terrain.

I really learned the system back when my brother, Brad, had just acquired his hunting camp in the Teton Wilderness of northwest Wyoming. The camp had been run by an old time, third generation outfitter. The fourth generation of the family had no interest in carrying on the tradition so my brother was able to step in and purchase the camp.

That fall we were guiding a party of the camp's repeat hunters, some of whom had hunted out of that camp for 15 years. After growing up in the outdoors and hunting elk all of our lives we thought we knew it all. One day a hunter asked me if we could go to Patterson Point to hunt deer. I drew a blank. Although I knew what area he was talking about, the lookout he mentioned was not familiar to me.

It was the third hunt of the season and there was a full moon. To make matters worse, the fall was dry and hot; and the animals were coming out just at dark. If you weren't within a few minutes of their grazing spot it would get dark leaving little or no time for a stalk. I needed a spot where I could easily glass the entire area. This way I could accurately mark the locations where they were coming out to feed. With this in mind I could be in position with my hunter before light the next morning.

I reluctantly agreed to have this flat-lander show me where to hunt. Believe me it was a real ego bender and I was secretly hoping he couldn't find the spot.

He led me to a small, timber-covered outcropping. It was perfectly concealed. If you didn't know exactly where you were going, you'd never realize what a great vantage point it was. As I slowly eased out onto the point, it was as if someone had pulled the shades back on a picture window. The whole country for miles around opened to view. We were easily able to see right into the small openings that we knew held elk and deer. Even below us, several open slides running down to the creek became visible. It was also the perfect shooting spot for game that fed out into the slides below. One thing about that day I'll always remember is looking down at my feet and seeing several corroded, spent 30-06 casings from seasons past.

That evening while glassing from the point, I thought about the other little spots I had glassed from over the years. They all had one thing in common, they offered me the opportunity to glass with the grain of the terrain. I would return to that secret lookout many times thereafter. It proved to be one of our most productive spots for locating trophy mule deer (Fig 4-3, pg. 69 and Fig. 4-4, pg. 70).

Glassing with the grain of the terrain allows you to clearly see across small openings, around ribbon cliffs, into strips of timber and small pockets. This is when you can make the most of your glassing time and improve your chances of picking up a trophy buck.

With experience you will be able to look at an area and see the grain of the terrain. Put simply, this means you are at the best angle to clearly see into the folds in the country. Sometimes just moving a few yards either way means the difference between being in the right place to see into pockets, or glassing from where your view is obstructed. You may not always want to glass across and down. Often it's more advantageous to be farther down country looking across and up a creek drainage.

In a new area, the best way to figure out the grain of the terrain is to simply move up and down the creek drainage. After a few tries, you will find the best spot from which to glass. This is where using my four-year plan comes into play...it takes some time to learn an area and find these special glassing spots. The more you move around, the greater your chances a smart buck will spot you and leave the country. Finding the perfect lookout is a trial and error process. There is nothing more helpful than becoming familiar with the country. Knowing how to glass with the grain is usually the reason one hunter can go into an area and spot game while another guy doesn't see much in the same drainage.

There is a mountain range west of Jackson Hole, Wyoming, where my brother, Rod, and I would hunt September mule deer in our youth. We had a running contest to see who could spot the most bucks in a given basin. I had a spot where I would frequently coyote out and look over the entire drainage. It was the best place to glass with the grain of the terrain. My brother would go down the ridgeline to another spot, but often times would not see half the bucks I would. I usually won the bet because I knew where to glass the basin with the grain of the terrain. The whole idea of glassing is to pick up on all the bucks in the area. Having the choice glassing spot will help you find the old buck who lives in a space only as big as your living room.

Glassing Techniques

I have a system of glassing for mule deer in the high country that was taught to me by my father, Gordon Eastman, when I first began hunting some 40 years ago. I begin glassing at the top of the peak even if it's nothing but granite. I work across and down, quickly checking the area for any animals that may be out in the open. When you are looking for mule deer, that first pass with your binoculars is the most important. Because a buck moves while he eats, the quicker I can effectively glass an area, the more efficient I will be in finding him before he drifts back into cover.

If on the first pass I don't see anything, I start over from the rocks at the top of the drainage. This time, I look with more detail around the small pockets I mentioned earlier. I also take a serious look at the edges of benches or ribbon cliffs. Big mule deer like to lie under a small conifer on the edge of a granite outcropping. The second pass is important because this is when I concentrate on pockets of timber, slides or any openings up against cover. This can be the most productive glassing because bucks are most likely to feed very close to their cover.

If I don't pick up anything on the second round, I'll start again this time looking into the small patches of timber and brush for a bedded or feeding buck. What I am doing is first looking in the most likely areas then going to the next hardest to spot and then the hardest. When glassing the bedding areas, you will have plenty of time without fear of the buck leaving the area. When glassing with the binoculars, I always have my spotting scope set up. I use it to look around the bedding areas and through the scrub pine pockets trying to pick up an antler or partial body form.

After the third scoping, I repeat the entire process again. Why? Because by the time you look again, a buck could be up and feeding right out in the open. As the sun moves, the light and shadows change. There

Tip: **4-5: 1. Edges of benches or ribbon cliffs. 2. Small patches of timber and brush for bedding or feeding bucks. Most hunters don't realize bucks make these areas their home.**

may be a buck lying under a tree that with the change of light suddenly becomes visible.

As you look at an area repeatedly, you develop a mental picture of every bush, rock and tree…you must memorize the terrain. Suddenly you may notice something, a form or object that looks different or out of place. It may be a shadow, a new shape or maybe even a slight movement. When you concentrate on it with your binoculars and spotting scope, sometimes it turns out to be a mule deer. To really become proficient at glassing you must learn how to quickly memorize the terrain on the first two passes.

After you spend some time hunting these high country mule deer, you will be able to recognize what I call "high probability" areas. (See photo above.) These can be areas under or next to trees, under an overhanging rock or on top of a 10,000 foot peak…anyplace a big buck is likely to make his nest. When a bedded buck is found in one of these areas, it then becomes a waiting game. If he isn't in position for a good stalk you must sit tight until he moves. This waiting game may take days.

When you spot mule deer feeding it is to your advantage to pay close

This high country mule deer buck in early September has a red appearance, making him easy to detect.

Tip: **4-6: Stay secluded and spot not only with binoculars but also a good lightweight spotting scope. I use a Leupold 25x50 because it is lightweight and has good light gathering capabilities for those early and late times of day. It's one of the keys to finding bucks. Over the years I've seen several bucks lying under this particular tree.**

attention to their body language. Many times I've seen feeding bucks continually looking back toward their bedding area. Sure enough, 15 or 20 minutes later a big mature trophy mule deer will step out into the open. A smart old buck will usually hang back while the others feed out first. When he feels everything is safe, he'll make his move out in the open. In these days of heavy hunting pressure, mature bucks will have a tendency to feed near their bedding areas and not venture too far up or down the basin or slide.

Take special notice if you see a group of bucks that keep looking off into the distance. Often a small group of 140- to 160-class bucks will feed out into the middle of a big bowl. If you glass late into the evening, chances are you'll spot a bigger buck a short distance from the main group. This is the reason I always make it a habit to stay out until it's too dark to see.

This reminds me of a story told to me by a fellow buck hunter, Steve Brewer. Steve took his cousin hunting into the wilderness around

Jackson Hole. (His cousin eventually killed one of the largest Trash Factor deer I've ever seen.) They spotted the buck feeding in a basin early in the morning and watched him lie down in a small conifer patch. The surrounding terrain was completely open. The two hunters spent the entire day trying to come up with a strategy to make a successful stalk on this giant buck.

Steve said it was very interesting to watch the behavior of this big mule deer in his bed. Every hour as the sun would move enough to begin shining on the buck, he would gently get up, make a little circle inside the conifer patch, and move back into the shade. This ritual went on all day as the sun moved across the sky. They finally devised a plan to put a stalk on the buck. Steve's cousin made his way down through a canyon and up the other side. He was able to sneak to within 350 yards to make the kill.

The thing to remember is that a big old buck does not like the sun...he prefers to hang in the shadows and shade. In my experience these bucks won't poke their heads out at all until the sun goes down far enough to create long shadows.

I'm sometimes asked how far away I set up to glass. When it comes to mule deer hunting, I stay as far away as possible. I don't want the buck to realize I'm hunting him. Using my spotting scope, I might start looking from a distance of two to three miles. I like being able to say I can spot a mule deer buck farther away than I could go in a day. Most of the time, taking a good buck involves the patience to find him and study his patterns before making a move (Fig. 4-6, pg. 75).

The hunter that rushes in usually comes out empty-handed. Unless you are pressured by other hunters, take your time and stay far enough away that the buck has no idea you're watching him.

In conclusion, high quality glass is important for finding deer but I think it's second to knowing where and how to glass. All the expensive binoculars in the world won't make a good spotter. Some guys will justify buying high dollar glass because less expensive products give them a headache after long hours of glassing. There is some truth to that but a good $300 pair of binoculars and a decent spotting scope combined with good glassing techniques will go a long way in spotting trophy mule deer.

Chapter 6

Early-Fall Hunting

During 35 years of hunting and guiding for high country mule deer, I have learned that bucks divide their summer and fall into two separate behavior periods. During each period they move into a specific terrain or home range. The season change in relation to the rut is what triggers this movement.

Late Summer Mode

This first section that I call the late summer mode generally runs from August 1 to about October 7. When the bucks are in their summer mode, you will find them on top of the peaks and high ridges. Why? Horse flies, deer flies, buffalo flies and mosquitoes love to feast on the soft, sensitive antlers in the velvet. High on top of the peaks and knife ridges the cool winds keep the pesky insects away. Another advantage is the early frost at 10,000 feet which usually occurs in mid-August and puts an end to these parasites.

During this period the bucks will move out at any time of day to feed. Many times I have been glassing a basin or snow slide at mid-afternoon and spotted several bucks out sunning themselves on a breezy slope. A rock ledge along the top of a basin is also an ideal area to glass for bucks lying in the sun. When mule deer are in their late summer mode, you need to spend the entire day glassing every possible feeding and bedding area.

It is during this period that the older mature bucks will hang together in bachelor groups. If you happen upon one of these groups, the sum of all those eyes and ears can make stalking much more challenging. Having several bucks milling around or trotting away can also make it difficult to pick the best trophy.

The ideal strategy is to slip into position and wait until the bucks move off to bed down for the day. It is very difficult for most hunters to lie quietly all day above a bedded buck waiting for him to stand or move out to feed. Most become impatient and attempt a stalk. Many good mule deer have escaped because the hunter just couldn't wait until evening. Remember, a smart old buck will have an escape route from his bed that is usually foolproof. If you wait until evening when the buck gets up to feed, it will generally provide you the opportunity

I hunted the Spear Point Peak buck for three years. To my knowledge no one ever took this deer.

to take a dead rest and make a clean shot on the unsuspecting trophy.

If it is dry in September, each of your steps often sounds like an elephant walking across a floor of peanut shells. As I've stated before, I think the mule deer has the best hearing of any North American big game specie. If a buck knows where you are, he has won the game. Many times they will stand until they pin down your location with their acute sense of hearing. This allows them to escape undetected.

Trying to jump a buck out of his bedding area as if hunting quail generally will not work on a high country deer. He will hide in a patch of conifers that is so small you swear nothing could be in there. You will have to almost step on him before he moves. Bucks have developed the ability to find holes to slip into where they'll watch you walk right by them. They become nervous only if you make eye contact with them. As long as you don't look directly into a buck's eyes, he will stay put. Look directly at him though, and watch out as he blows out without even looking back. If you don't believe me, watch the Mule Deer Stalker III video that documents this exact behavior.

Back when I was outfitting I had a spot that was noted for holding good bucks. The first time I saw the Spear Point Peak buck was when I was driving the timber on the back side of the peak one September day.

Note: **6-1: Spear Point Peak is an area that many trophy mule deer called home. (1.) I pushed the big buck out of that patch into the hunters waiting (2.) on the flat below. Unfortunately they missed and he disappeared (see story). (3.) Many times I have found bucks living on these shelves overlooking the creek bottom 500 feet below. By staying back and watching you can pick out the bucks as they move out to feed. I have cut off bucks as they ran around this peak trying to escape.**

Chris Lacey
1997
©

With two hunters positioned below the crest I worked around and through the timber. I knew if there was a buck there he would blow out and run right by those guys on his way to the heavy cover of the creek drainage below. Just as I had predicted I soon heard shooting and then silence.

It didn't look good as I made my way down to the hunters. Their heads shaking back and forth spelled misfortune. Both had missed shots as the buck trotted by at less than 100 yards. I immediately knew both guys had over-shot the deer and didn't touch a hair on him. "Where did he go?" I asked. Both hunters agreed he ran out about 400 yards and just disappeared. He hadn't even made it to the creek, it was as if the earth just swallowed him up.

As hard as it was to believe, it sure sounded like he had jumped into a crevasse on the opposite edge of a big granite flat. Making our way down and slipping up to the 6-foot hole, I peeked over the edge. I had one hunter on the right and the other on my left with their guns shouldered and ready. Looking carefully over the edge, I could barely see the buck's ears as they moved in all directions listening intently to our movements.

He had had enough of us and couldn't stand it any longer. Suddenly he sprang straight up out of the crevasse, landing on the opposite side in one jump. Now only 10 feet away from us he was headed for the cover of the creek below. The hunters managed to get off one quick shot at the buck, but they were so startled their bullets went right over his head. In five jumps he was in the cover of the creek bottom.

The Spear Point Peak buck wasn't seen again until the next fall. It was very frustrating for me to watch hunters miss that huge deer twice at such close distance. Back then, there just weren't too many guys who could really hunt at this extremely high altitude. Either they were out of shape and couldn't get their wind back, or the sight of 30-inch plus deer would just get the best of them.

So often hunters assume when they jump a deer he immediately leaves the country. Actually he will usually head for the first patch of cover and hide until you are long gone before moving out completely. The most ineffective way to hunt a big buck is to walk around in hopes of jumping and spotting him. Remember, if a mule deer knows you're around more often than not he just stays hid until you have left the area.

Tracking bucks in this rocky country is fruitless without the presence of snow. A buck leaves no tracks to follow on solid granite rock. Learning his behavior patterns or where he goes after he has been spooked takes years of hunting the area.

A high country buck does have some habits the smart hunter can capitalize upon. My experience has taught me that a buck will come back to the same high country summer grounds year after year.

When I was much younger, I hunted a wise old buck living in a high mountain basin not more then 10 miles from downtown Jackson, Wyoming. I first discovered the buck when I jumped him from a secluded ribbon cliff while working my way down to the bottom of a basin. Every year for the next three years the old buck would show up in the

same basin. Year after year he could be found lying on the same bench overlooking the surrounding terrain. From that position he had several escape routes from which to choose.

Approaching from the top, the loose shale rock would give me away. When coming in from the sides or bottom I would be spotted from 600 yards away.

On opening day of the second year I tried walking into his conifer bedding area from the top only to hear the unmistakable thump, thump of him escaping into the distance. I got only a brief glimpse of his rack as he left. The buck was about 27 inches wide but the most appealing part of his antler configuration was definitely his mass that carried out well to the ends of the points. He had developed several extra points branching from his back tines.

After jumping him out, the old buck disappeared for the rest of the season, going to a secondary living area that I could never find. Other bucks would reappear in several days after being spooked, but not him, once he had blown out he was gone for the entire season. I spent a long cold winter thinking of a way to outsmart the buck and successfully get to his bedding spot. I finally came to the conclusion the only possible way to get a good shot would be to slip down on him from above without making any noise.

After a third year, I got used to the sound of his thumping hooves as he again made good his escape. The situation was becoming personal in a hurry. That heavy, 27-inch, 9x9 was a monster to a 16 year-old trophy hunter with a strong case of buck fever. During those years we could hunt through the rut and up to the end of December. I would always get into some good mule deer hunting late in the season, but there was something about that early season buck that intrigued me. I really wanted to take him before he got too old and disappeared as they so often do.

By the fourth year, I had finally wised up. On opening day of the early mule deer season, I hoped the old buck was back in his favorite bed once again. A blanket of wet September snow had fallen during the night and as I arrived at the edge above the basin, an idea hit me. I removed my boots and began sneaking down the hill, making sure every step was carefully placed. It took 15 minutes to cover the 100 yards to the dozing buck. My wool socks were soaked and my feet were so cold feeling the terrain underfoot was an impossibility. I remember thinking that at any minute I would hear the familiar thud, thud as the buck left the country. As I got closer, more and more doubt crept into my mind. He must not be there or he would have jumped up by now. Perhaps being so old, the buck had died during the winter with its 50 below zero temperatures and above normal snowfall.

Finally, the tips of the buck's back tines came into view and my heart began to pound out of my chest. After three years, I was right on top of him. Two more delicate steps and I could see his rack and head. Inching forward, I could see of the buck's shoulder and back as he lay facing downhill completely unaware of my presence. Raising the Springfield 30-06 to my shoulder I placed the crosshairs right on the top of his shoulder. Slowly I clicked off the safety. The metallic sound caused him to jump straight into the air like a rocket. His head swiveled up looking me straight in the eye. I squeezed off the shot as he struggled to gain his footing. The entire event took no more than three seconds. As suddenly as it had begun, it ended. His lifeless body slid down the snowy

6-2: This old buck, the smartest I have ever taken, took three years of hunting to harvest.

6-3: Taking a nontypical buck like this at age 17 was a thrill that stays with me to this day.

Tip: **6-4: A good lookout gives you the advantage of being able to look over many miles of terrain. This was one of my favorite spots, (remember not to silhouette yourself as I am doing for the benefit of the camera). If you do, a buck will spot you from miles away and then become nocturnal or leave the area for his secondary nest in some rugged hole where you won't find him.**

slope and piled up against a patch of scrub pines beneath his bed.

The buck was definitely beyond the peak of his life span. His right eye was gone, probably having been gored out in a fight during the previous year's rut. He had battle scars on his face and a knot atop his large Roman nose. Though his antlers had regressed from the first year, he was still the largest buck I had taken until that time. The local Game and Fish biologist aged the toothless old buck at better than 10 years of age, he more than likely wouldn't have made it through the winter (Fig. 6-2 and Fig 6-3, pg. 84).

What made that hunt so unforgettable was being able to finally outsmart the old buck after so many years. His habit of coming back to the same summer bedding area year after year proved to be his Achilles heel. I have found over the years that if a buck is disturbed he will often leave for his backup area that can be in a completely different drainage several miles away.

Strategies For Getting A Shot

Make no mistake, the terrain where these bucks live during the early fall is the rockiest, steepest, nastiest piece of real estate you've ever laid eyes upon. In fact, this country is so rough, it is often overlooked by many trophy hunters as being uninhabitable for mule deer.

If you use the coyoting out method (see chapter four) of hunting, you will be watching several basins simultaneously, looking for that one in one-hundred trophy buck. Each basin is unique and can have several areas that could possibly hold deer. The lower ends of these basins will typically have some dark timber cover. Bucks feel safe in these basins knowing that one jump will put them into the safety of the pines. Glassing your way up, don't forget to look under and on top of the ribbon cliffs that often encircle a basin's uppermost reaches. Finally, always check out the ledges high above the basin where a buck can lie with his back against a rock wall overlooking the whole creek drainage.

Picking up a buck moving to his bedding area early in the morning can be a real advantage. Large portions of these high basins are wide open, you can usually watch a buck feed all the way back to his bed. However this is only half the battle, now you need to locate his escape routes. The importance of knowing how he can escape cannot be overstated.

Near the head of one of the creeks I used to hunt, a peak surrounded by sparse patches of timber rose from a solid granite bench (Fig 6-1, pg. 79. Bucks loved to lie in the fine black volcanic sand that was found in the area. They were very hard to pick out and as I glassed the area I would spot more and more bucks the closer I looked.

One time when I had a hunter with me, we slipped over to where several bucks were bedded. I was able to get the hunter right up on the sleeping bucks. He took his time and slowly squeezed off a shot that went high right over their backs. It was like an explosion. Mass confusion ensued as racks bounced in every direction. Every time the excited hunter would pull down on a buck another buck would appear in his scope. It all happened within a few seconds and the deer vanished around the base of Spear Point Peak. I gathered up the rattled hunter and headed around to the opposite side. The hunter contested that the bucks had gone around the other side. I just said, "come on," and ran him around to a point 180 degrees opposite of where the bucks had last disappeared. Positioning him with a dead rest, I told him to wait until the deer showed up and I would pick out the best buck in the bunch. Sure enough, they soon appeared walking in single file toward where we were waiting in ambush. My were they surprised! This time the hunter was more relaxed and was easily able to take one of the larger bucks in the group. The point of this is, I knew from experience the deer would circle around and come in behind us and end up in almost the same area they had been bedded. However after a second encounter, they headed out single file over a saddle into another creek drainage.

Remember, in the morning a buck will usually first lie down in a secondary bedding area and watch his back trail for at least 30 minutes before moving on to the security of the primary bedding area. This doesn't happen all the time but you still must give a buck enough time to settle into his day bed before you slip into his territory. If you carefully glass the area above a buck's day bed, chances are you will see a faint trail leading out over the top of the basin and into the next drainage. This is the buck's escape route. I use my written journal to describe the surrounding area, so when I get over there I have a better idea of how the country lies and where any possible escape routes might be.

Once these escape routes are identified, located and documented, two hunters can easily push a buck into an ambush. Positioning one hunter inconspicuously within shooting distance of the escape route, the other can slowly move from the bottom up toward the bedded deer. Don't make too much noise, just slowly ease up the mountain as if you were out on a hike. Most of the time, the deer will get up and use his escape route to sneak away undetected by the lower hunter. The second hunter positioned above and near the trail will have the perfect opportunity for a good shot as the buck tries to slip by.

One time while guiding, I rode out to the edge of a slope that was covered with scattered patches of scrub pines and contained many rock slides. Carefully glassing, I spotted a buck lying in a patch of timber over a mile away. With just his head visible, this smart old buck could watch the trails below him for the slightest sign of activity. He had the perfect escape route…all he had to do was quickly ascend to the top of the ridge using the strip of scrub pines as cover all the way to the top.

I outsmarted this mule deer by going all the way around the mountain and setting my hunter up on the ridge above the timber patch. I then returned to the lower end of the slope where I knew the buck could see me. I started slowly up the trail. Sure enough he got up and tried to slip out through the top, keeping that patch of timber between him and I the entire time. With his attention riveted on me, he slowly and quietly walked right into my hunter on the crest of the ridge.

If you use this strategy, be sure your partner doesn't move in too close to the buck or the escape trail. Keep your distance and be careful not to make too much noise. The last thing you want is the buck to panic and blow out at 30 miles per hour. If your partner slips along carefully and sets up correctly, the buck will try to carefully sneak out by way of his escape route right into your ambush. This is one advantage of hunting with a partner. Many trophy hunters however, prefer to go it alone rather than put up with a partner.

Mule deer have a great sense of smell. More than one big buck has left the country over a nostril full of human scent. It is, of course, always imperative to have the wind with you in all your hunting plans.

In the mountains, thermals will raise havoc with your stalking efforts. The swirling and changing winds can be a constant disadvantage to you. Sometimes when stalking a bedded or feeding buck, the thermals will suddenly change and he is gone. I carry a small squeeze bottle of powder to constantly test the air movement. If it changes, I try to compensate for it by changing stalking directions. If the thermals become

Tip: **6-5: I took this buck in a patch of timber in a high mountain basin. His buddy had a wider spread but would not have scored as well. I watched them for several days figuring out which escape routes they might use. Even then, the bigger buck just about slipped out undetected. He let his buddy run while he lay there waiting for me to walk past him in pursuit of the other deer. When I saw him, we made eye contact and he jumped and ran. I was able to take him with one shot at only 75 feet. Remember escape routes, you need to know them before attempting a stalk on a buck's nest.**

too bad, wait until the afternoon sun is down before stalking. At that time the basin will often become calm because the air movement is then directed up the mountain. The reason is, the warmer air rises up toward the cold sky. The opposite generally happens in the morning, the warm air flows down into the bottom of the cold shady basin. Through the use of a journal over time, you can permanently document these air flows in specific basins and drainages.

If hunting alone, the best strategy is to slip into position, wait patiently and let the buck make the first move. However, in some areas your only option is to make a stalk on the buck. Don't think that because you can't see into his bedding area, he can't see out. Even though a group of pines might appear to obstructing his view, most of the time a smart buck can see in all directions…he has no blind side. Some of these beds are hundreds of years old and three feet deep from generation after generation of bedding mule deer bucks. It is a strategically placed home that is passed on from one generation to the next.

Take your time and be patient as you make your stalk. Unless you're hunting in an area with other hunters, you have all day to pull off this surprise package. Remember, if a buck hears, smells or sees anything out of the ordinary, he's gone.

One common stalking mistake is to assume that because a buck goes into a timber patch alone, he is the only buck there. Usually there will be more than one buck; they prefer to lie down together facing in different directions for obvious reasons.

Also, if there is more than one buck they may not all get up at the same time to begin feeding. Seeing a single buck browsing around a scrub pine doesn't necessarily mean he is alone. That is why glassing and studying every inch of a scrub pocket is so critical. It gives you the chance to pick up any other bucks that may be hidden in the area.

Hunting trophy mule deer alone allows you the opportunity to come up with some interesting angles to fool a smart old buck one on one. Here is a trick that can be used when a buck is found bedded in a small patch of scrub timber. If you have a good arm, try throwing a few rocks over the top of the buck so that they land below him. Many times the buck will get nervous and try sneaking up and out the top where you are waiting in ambush.

Early fall hunting is the best time to find high country mule deer bucks. It allows you the pleasure of hunting in good weather when mule deer are still in their lazy, summer behavior mode. There are many early high country hunts throughout the western states that offer great opportunities combined with low hunting pressure.

Remember when hunting the high country, whether it's Colorado, Idaho or Wyoming, the best time is from September 1 through the first week of October. It is the golden time for finding mule deer bucks in bachelor groups. This is when they're in their summer mode and can be found out feeding at any time during the day.

One evening I was glassing in the head of Fox Creek when a total of 18 bucks fed out of a small patch of scrub pines. They had been lying in an area no bigger than an average sized house. That is the most mule deer bucks I have seen in one bachelor group. But finding three or four in a group is a common occurrence at this time of the season. Hunting during the second portion of the fall is the most difficult. If you can get a permit for the early fall hunt, your chances of finding a trophy buck are greatly improved.

Chapter 7

Mid-Fall Hunting

The second mule deer period is what I call the mid-fall mode. This runs from October 7 to about the first week of November. Most hunting seasons throughout the West are scheduled for this time of year, it is cooler then and more than likely there's even a little snow in the high country. In fact, some of the more secluded high mountain basins may be full of snow and most of the passes will be blocked by then. For many hunters, this is the only season available to hunt mule deer.

However when you look at what a mule deer buck is doing during this time, it's obvious the hunter is at an extreme disadvantage. A buck's mindset will change in a way that makes him difficult to hunt. In some areas like Colorado's Las Alamos Valley, the big bucks pull down off the high basins into the deep timber. They aren't seen again until they reappear on the valley floor for the November rut. By then, the hunting season is long gone. The only time you have an opportunity to harvest one of these bucks is during one of the September early high country hunts.

Bucks in Wyoming's Salt River Range behave in much the same way. One of these huge bucks is occasionally taken during the combination elk/mule deer hunt in October by hunters driving the timber for elk.

Thorough research is the key to taking a big buck during this time of year. You have to know about secluded basins where bucks will hang back in the timber until the rut starts. These are typically located in areas where deer don't have to migrate over high divides to get to their breeding/winter grounds. The weather is critical during this period. A sudden snowstorm can act as a trigger sending the bucks to lower conifer areas, or even over a divide and out of your hunting area. The number one factor that effects mule deer movement is weather. If they guess wrong if could mean their death.

I remember one time when my two brothers were guiding for an outfitter in Jackson Hole, Wyoming. They were trying to take a good non-typical that hung around a particular snow slide on a 10,000-foot peak. Finally, the last part of the season came and the buck was still making his home in that slide. November 15 was the last day of the season and waist deep snow had piled up on the peak. My brother, Rod, could watch the buck in his spotting scope trying to feed in the snow slide. However, there was just too much snow for him to get over to the buck.

7-1: My father, Gordon Eastman, took this buck during a snowy early November hunt in Wyoming. Remember to key in on the weather throughout the season, it is the number one event that triggers changes in a mule deer buck's routine. His whole life is dictated by fending off weather and being able to move to the winter range unrestricted by deep snow. I record all movements in my journal and have a small thermometer pinned to my coat. A day by day record of the weather is invaluable and even in the early fall will help you pattern trophy mule deer movements.

All winter we talked about that good buck and wondered if Rod could get a shot at him the following fall. The September opener found Rod in the slide looking for the buck. With no luck he elected to move over to the back side of the peak and check out some new country. Walking through the slide he found the bones of the big buck laying in a 75-foot circle with the rack in the middle. The buck waited too long and was trapped in the slide. We often wondered if a winter snow slide had come down sweeping him to his death. Unfortunately coyotes had broken the skull so it couldn't be officially scored for B&C.

I make it a habit to write down weather conditions and temperatures in my journal (a small thermometer like cross-country skiers use is clipped to the zipper of my coat). You may be surprised how sensitive mule deer are to changing weather. I think it's the number one factor influencing their behavior in the high country.

In some areas like the Teton Wilderness in northern Wyoming, the deer will winter 70 miles from their summer area. If snow comes in the high country at the end of September, they head for their wintering areas. Crossing the Continental Divide on their trek, they will often hang up on the other side just below timber line for as long as the weather holds. Then as the snow accumulates, they drift on down to the desert country below. You must know the migration patterns of the deer if you are hunting this time of year. If not, you could end up hunting in an area where the deer have already left for the winter range. This information can be gathered from the local Game & Fish Department. However, to receive detailed information you need to talk to other sources such as local residents in the area.

Deer in each area will have their own unique patterns of movement. There is one particular area in Wyoming that has excellent potential for trophy high mountain mule deer. When the October 15 season opens, the snow is waist deep at 10,000 feet and the deer have all left for their transition areas to await the rut. I feel sorry for the poor nonresident who draws a permit for this unit and heads into the high country!

Before applying for any high mountain mule deer hunt during this period, there are several important questions you must ask a local biologist: Which route will the deer travel to reach their winter range? How much snow accumulation is needed to trigger the migration? Over the last five years, what has been the general time frame for the deer migration?

It is during this late October period that a buck will only come out at night to feed. He will change his routine and suddenly become nocturnal. I believe several factors come into play to influence his change in behavior. Number one, it is now that time of the season right before the rut and the bucks have stored up their winter fat and put on a heavy coat, somewhat like you having to wear your winter clothing around when it's not quite winter weather. Avoiding the intense fall sun becomes a habit, perhaps even an obsession at this time. Second, because he isn't exerting much energy at this time a buck doesn't need as much vegetation to sustain him. Because of the frosty nights, the vegetation has changed in its nutrition content. Deer now must key on different food sources, particularly ones that are found closer to their bedding area. Lastly, the buck goes through a personality change...he develops a loner type attitude that is conducive to the approaching rut.

Because the bucks aren't very active, you have to be able to wait them

out and stay in their area without them being aware of your presence. Coyoting out is a hunting style that can be used very successfully this time of year. A buck might feed for only 30 minutes each day before returning to the shady timber to await the rut. You have to constantly glass to pick up a buck during his brief feeding period. That rough, dark timber at the bottom of the basin becomes his new home. Trying to slip in on him while he is in the timber is next to impossible.

The sun is getting lower in the sky and the snow slides on the north slopes have more daytime shade. Bucks will move into them until the snow forces them down or out of the area completely. Even with these shady snow slides they still limit their activity to brief periods of feeding during the late evening or night. It is really important when coyoting out at this time of year to stay in one area for an extended period of time. It takes more time to find and pattern a buck in his mid-fall mode. He is only coming out once every several days, usually right at dark.

Under these circumstances it is very easy to get discouraged when very few bucks are seen in the open. This is typically when most guys start driving timber pockets and north facing slopes. During this period driving deer can produce bucks, but usually a large old deer will just double back around you and slip away undetected. If you do drive a timber pocket, I suggest you position a hunter in back where you started the drive just in case a trophy buck does double back on you.

One type of terrain that I like to drive is a slide with timber on both sides extending to the top of the ridge. A buck will climb out, keeping himself in the timber until he hits the top and goes over the saddle of a ridge into the next basin. It is most advantageous to place one hunter at the top in the funnel of the saddle. A real problem can be encountered if the driving hunters don't take it slow, they can make the buck blow out over the ridge at top speed. Trying to shoot a buck that is racing past you full blast is almost impossible. Driving deer becomes an art, moving up the mountain at a slow pace. Remember, a buck that has been driven several times will get to the point where he absolutely will not come out at all. I have watched them simply move to the side in the cover and let you walk right on past. Remember in this day and age mule deer bucks of age have nerves of steel. They will lie without moving until you just about step on them. So many hunters underestimate a buck's ability to stay hidden while you walk around in his area. Learning to be patient, waiting and glassing without been detected by the big buck are steps toward a good deer.

Driving can become an effective way to kick out a buck but too much will sour a big trophy to the technique all together. Knowing when and where to drive comes with hunting experience. Learning the movements of the deer and areas that hold bucks becomes crucial knowledge for this type of hunting. Going into the region before hunting season and locating the bucks is a good strategy. However, if you're there in August, I guarantee by mid-October those bucks will have split up and moved into different areas awaiting the rut.

A trophy hunter must realize these bucks move around into slides and conifer areas. With this in mind you can now concentrate your efforts on those areas during your October hunt. Each year your knowledge will grow until knowing what the deer will do under different conditions becomes second nature to you. The prospect of finding good bucks will become easier in those areas you have spent adequate time observing.

This 190 buck has good fronts and bad backs. His G-4 and main beam are exceptionally long, unfortunately the G-3 branches too high off the G-2 (refer to pg. 134) Even at that the buck scores well over 190 gross typical.

Chapter 8

Pockets and Slides

Where do you find high mountain mule deer? Most hunters don't look in the proper terrain. They have read too many how-to books about bucks that live in the conifer-aspen transition areas. The secret of finding big, high mountain mule deer is finding isolated pockets, basins and slides that are off the beaten path. High pockets and basins have everything a buck needs to live throughout the summer and early fall...isolation, good feed and usually a small water source nearby. These factors allow him to reach middle age where he can potentially attain his best antler growth.

Several years ago, I was hunting one of these isolated basins for mule deer. On the opposite side of the pocket was a 10,500-foot peak. Until that day, I had never really glassed the top 500 feet of the mountain, which was mostly composed of granite rock with a sparse scattering of four-foot high scrub pines. I had always concentrated my glassing on the lower sections of the peak, the strips of timber and pockets where I'd seen bucks on several occasions (Fig. 8-1, pg. 99).

That night a wet skiff of snow had blanketed the tops of the peaks. Merely by chance, the next morning I started to glass the very top of the high peak. There in the snow, I detected a faint trail angling up from the scrub pines and over the top. The trail was so faint I would have never picked it out without the snow accenting its location.

Knowing there had to be a buck somewhere in that scrub pine patch, I spent the rest of the day glassing with my spotting scope. Finally at five o'clock that evening, a high mountain buck slipped out of the timber patch. With the snow providing a perfect background, I carefully studied his rack. The main beams were over 26 inches long with an inside spread of at least 25 inches. Even without the cheaters, he had a solid 30-inch outside main frame spread. That buck was definitely pushing 190 gross!

With his head lowered, he moved slowly up the faint trail and disappeared over the back side of the peak. What a beautiful sight his skylined rack made as he topped out! I knew he would spend the night feeding in a small basin on the other side of the mountain.

Back at camp I told my brother, Rod, the buck probably followed that trail into his feeding area every evening. The next day Rod and a hunter slipped into the isolated basin to wait for evening. Just like clockwork,

8-1: The big buck lived in this patch of timber (1.) all fall moving through the pass during the night to feed in a basin on the back side (2.). A small trail was detected after a light skiff of snow had fallen one night.

Illustration on the left: The buck lived totally undetected by me for many years in the conifer patch shown by the arrow (1.) in the photo above.

the buck appeared at dusk for his evening feeding. One well-placed bullet took the old boy down (Fig. 8-2, pg. 100).

I'm convinced that buck had been following the same routine his entire adult life. A smart buck will go to extreme measures to avoid being harassed. This particular buck had found an area that was devoid of human activity. Finding a pocket that is overlooked or too rugged for the majority of hunters is one of the best secrets for getting a chance at a trophy. I can't stress enough the importance of finding spots like this that are rarely hunted.

Tip: **8-2a: A pocket like this offers you a chance to see a good buck. The timber to the right is an ideal spot for a mule deer nest. Also look into the patches of timber to the left where bucks lay in the shade.**

8-2: The 190 class buck lived on that peak in the isolated basin undetected for many years.

Tip: **8-2b: 1. Look into those high conifer patches for bedded bucks. 2. An ideal spot for bucks to call home because with very little effort he can move over a pass and into a different creek drainage. 3. Anywhere you have a patch of timber you could find mule deer living. Escape routes are important to know and recognize.**

8-2c: I took this 31-inch buck in a high mountain basin where he was living in a scrub pine conifer patch.

8-2d: Look at the rocks and rough terrain around this deer. Most hunters wouldn't think a deer could live here.

Tip: **8-2e: The arrows show pockets where I have found bucks living during the early fall. The rougher and more isolated, the better these deer like it.**

Tip: **8-2f: These areas have no major trails so I have to bushwhack my way into them, but I guarantee you will find bucks living there. Once you find a buck's nest, you can go back every year and find deer there. In your journal, plot your movements and where you see deer.**

Tip: **8-3: Slides are a type of terrain where you will find bucks living. Most are very steep and hunters find glassing them difficult and resist looking there. Steep slides can, however, produce good mule deer.**

Hunting Snow Slides

High country snow slides are overlooked by many trophy mule deer hunters (Fig. 8-3, pg. 104). A snow slide is a natural chute where a buildup of snow in the winter causes avalanches. In the dead of winter the snow finally comes crashing down taking out most of the big trees in its path, leaving only scrub pines and brush. On both sides of these chutes you will typically find timber-covered knife ridges that run parallel with the slide from top to bottom (Fig. 8-4. pg. 106).

There are several reasons mule deer like these areas. The number one reason is the lush feed that grows there, (most slides also have an active spring along their edge). These slides are usually on north facing slopes where, during the summer and early fall, temperatures can be 10 degrees cooler than their southern counterparts. A buck prefers to live in these isolated, cool areas. Secondly, the timbered ridges on either side offer secure, well hidden bedding areas. I have watched mule deer bucks spend an entire fall without ever leaving a slide, and why should they…it offers everything they need to survive.

One reason many hunters don't like to hunt snow slides is that they are perhaps the hardest of all high mountain terrain to glass. Because of the vegetation, you have to take a position straight across from a slide to glass it effectively. This might mean glassing from a distance of up to

8-5a: Carl with a buck taken out of a slide. We watched the buck for several days before making a move on him. With his cheater he was almost 30 inches wide. Remember, slides do produce bucks and they are commonly overlooked by hunters.

several miles. Oftentimes on north facing slides the flat light and dark shade make it hard to pick up a buck. After you find a buck, low light conditions and long glassing distances can make it extremely difficult to accurately judge his rack size.

Snow slides often have areas of chest-high brush and young scrub trees that make it tough to spot a buck. Glassing one of these brush patches becomes very demanding mentally...you literally have to pick the area apart looking for a piece of a mule deer. After a good buck is

Tip: **8-4: 1. Glassing snow slides from this distance will give you an edge because the buck doesn't have a clue you are around. Most of the time an old buck goes undetected by hunters and lives out his life with little hunting pressure.**

spotted, the stalk can be equally challenging. Moving along the edge of a slide everything looks the same and keeping your bearings straight becomes difficult. Be patient and don't hurry, you are going up against your quarry at close range. Here you lack the luxury of using distance as a buffer as you do when hunting the high peaks and open basins. It's no wonder an old buck loves this type of terrain.

Deer that have fed into the brush are difficult to get a bead on. Many times I have gone after a snow slide buck only to be rewarded by the sound of his antlers raking against the vegetation as he made his escape. I have even tried to drive these slides, but the older bucks will usually double back and get away. Sometimes you can slip in and wait until dusk and then try a stalk into the wind. Perhaps the best way to get on one of these snow slide bucks is to get above him and stalk down. You have to really know the terrain and have the buck in just the right position for this tactic to work. Having the deer in an area that has some open space is an advantage to you.

I remember one smart old buck that fell to this strategy. On several occasions we had seen him feeding in a snow slide along with several 150 B&C bucks. Unfortunately he was never in a position where we could get a hunter on him. The terrain was very steep and I knew from experience a stalk on him would be impossible. Consequently, every three or four days I would ride to the top of the peak just at dusk and look over to check on him. Barely visible above the tops of the brush you could see his antler tips moving as he and his buddies fed in the slide. They always stayed in the thick brush until well past shooting time.

Finally, two weeks later as I performed the evening ritual of checking on the buck, I caught the old boy feeding out on a bench just above the protection of the scrub pines and brush. The accompanying hunter made a great shot on the buck and added a good 170 net mule deer to his collection. By waiting the buck out and not pushing him from his living area, this hunt had a successful conclusion. It just took time and patience until the buck finally made a mistake that I was able to capitalize upon. So many times guys get antsy and tromp into the buck's area in hopes of jump shooting him. Ninety-nine percent of the time it doesn't work.

A variation of this strategy is to coyote out all night on a knife ridge next to a slide. This may put you in a good position for an ambush as he moves to his bedding area the next morning. If you can sit tight all night and not make any type of impact on the area, you will be able to surprise the buck come morning. He isn't accustomed to having a hunter bedded right there with him Fig. 8-5a. pg. 105).

Despite all the negative aspects of hunting snow slides, they are well worth the trouble. Some of the biggest bucks I have ever seen were living in these areas. If the truth was known, snowslides hold more good bucks than the basins or ribbon cliff areas. In my experience, if a buck is pushed out of a basin by hunting pressure, he will usually move to a north slope where he can hide out and live in these rough snow slides. In slide areas there are many dark timber patches in which to bed and keep a low profile throughout the fall.

Ribbon Cliffs and Rock Benches

The winter before my third year of outfitting trophy mule deer hunts, we had a bad winter kill. You couldn't find a good buck to save yourself. When one of these winters comes along it takes its toll on the yearlings and rut-weakened older bucks. This makes finding a good mature deer the following fall seem like mission impossible. I had looked in all the normal pockets and slides but was able to locate only a few middle-aged bucks.

On the third day of the hunt, we were in a drainage where I had never before taken hunters. The country was very rough and looking at it you'd think every loose rock in the entire mountain range had ended up in this particular basin. It didn't have much for timber and the sides had only ribbon cliffs, one after the other going from the basin floor to the top of the peaks (Fig. 8-7, pg. 109). To make matters worse there were numerous cliffs and rock slides throughout the basin. This country was treacherous even for an experienced high mountain hunter. It would be very easy to get rimmed in, causing difficulty getting back to the basin floor. You had better know the way out come evening or you could find yourself waiting until the next morning on a rocky ledge.

Glassing with my 20 power spotting scope, I finally found a buck lying on a ribbon cliff with nothing but air below the outcrop he used for a bed (Fig. 8-8, pg. 109). Looking at his snow white face, you could tell he had gone through many hard years and was on the downhill side of his life. I knew I'd have to get my hunter above the buck to get a decent shot.

After hours of working our way around the basin and carefully stalking through several steep rock slides I told the hunter we still had a hard slow climb ahead. Considering the limited number of deer we had seen during the hunt, he elected to go on.

Climbing at 10,000 feet is a physically draining experience even for someone who is reasonably acclimated. Trying to get a hunter who comes from sea level into position to kill a buck under these conditions becomes a real trick. I have found if you take your time, climbing a few yards then resting, you can pace yourself for an all-day climb. Too many guys try to bite off the whole mountain in a race to get to their destination. My advice for the hunter climbing and stalking in the high country is, "Take it slow, it's not a race."

After a five-hour climb we were finally in position above the bedded buck. I instructed the hunter to hold right behind the deer's shoulder. The shot echoed through the basin, as the bullet struck the shoulder directly. The buck jumped to his feet, turned and looked right at us. I heard the bolt of 30-06 slam shut and out of the corner of my eye saw the hunter raise the rifle to his shoulder for another shot. Suddenly the buck jumped from the ledge as if to commit suicide!

The sound of antler cracking up against granite rose from far below the cliff where the buck had been bedded. Walking out to the edge with a knot in my stomach I carefully looked over, the buck was piled up dead 100 feet below.

It may be hard for some people to believe, but over the years I have

Tip: **8-7: The ribbon cliffs will hold bucks and you need to glass them over and over again. Just because you don't see a buck on the first several passes, don't give up. He may feed out of the sun to a place where you can see him.**

8-8: Bucks like flat areas with some timber and a view. Looking over the drainage is a habit of mule deer. Always look at the spots that offer a good view of the surrounding country.

witnessed bucks leaping off cliffs on three different occasions. I don't know if they get confused and think they can get away or maybe they actually commit suicide! One of the bucks jumped off a cliff and landed on all fours, luckily for him there was a foot and half of snow to cushion his leap. In two more jumps he was gone. Another buck leaped off and landed in a rock slide below, breaking his back. If I hadn't seen it, I would never have believed bucks would jump from cliffs like that.

That 180 gross B&C buck turned out to be the best we took all that fall. You know, he didn't break a single point in the fall. His antlers were only scratched and scarred up a bit from the fall into the rocks. There have been times when a buck has fallen down a chute or slide and broken points or even whole main beams off! Any trophy hunter holds his breath when a big buck takes a leap onto a rock pile like that.

It took an entire day to backpack him out of that hole to the horses above. As difficult as my experience sounds, this is the type of terrain you have to hunt if you want to find good quality high country trophies nowadays. You can bet the older mature bucks will be found in the most rugged terrain in the area.

I usually glass the tops of ribbon cliffs looking for bedding areas. Typically these cliffs will wander along the basin's steep side walls. Often times there will be pine trees growing on top of the rock outcroppings (Fig. 8-9, pg. 112). These scrub pines above the ribbon cliffs offer concealed areas where the bucks will bed. From there, they can look over a lot of country and the only way you can get to them is from the top.

By glassing during mid-day when they're in their beds you can sometimes pick up the location of a mule deer. Because it is so steep and inaccessible, hunters overlook this type of terrain thereby passing up some of the best areas for big deer. Personally, I think taking a buck from an area like this is a physical and mental challenge that can only be matched by a few animals in North America (Fig. 8-10, pg. 112).

Tip: **8-8a, 8-8b, 8-8c: Look at the 36-inch bucks on the next page and you will see tape is used to keep the antlers together. They all fell from cliffs and broke their racks. Whether they jumped intentionally or just fell, the important thing to remember is mule deer live in extremely high cliffy areas. Look in the steepest country you can find.**

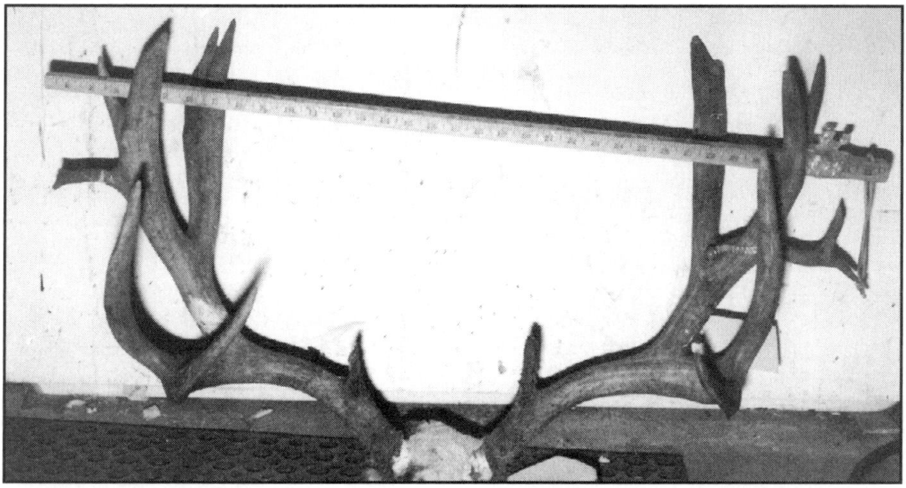

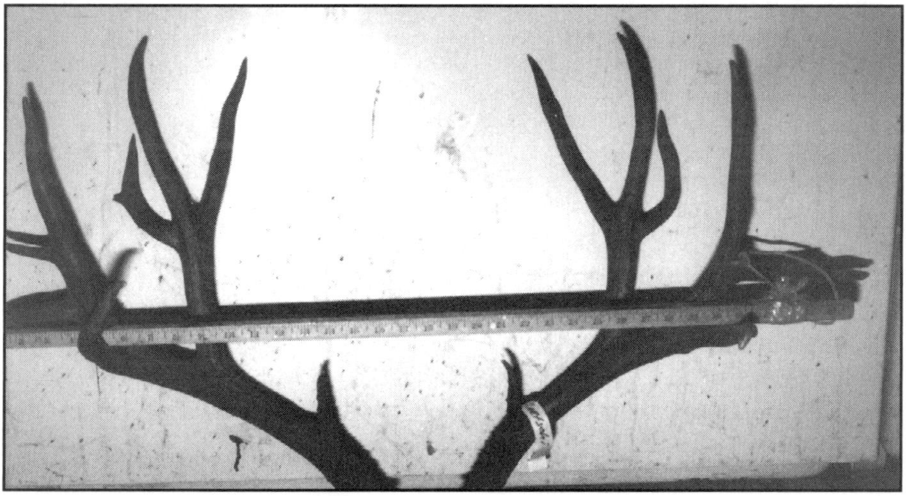

8-9: High granite shelves are good areas for bucks. Even with the steepness of the country, mule deer like this terrain and live through the early fall here above 10,000 feet.

Note: **8-10: In these areas with the arrows, I have personally taken or had hunters take good bucks. It is so steep that at times after shooting bucks, they rolled down the mountain several hundred yards, landing in a patch of conifers. Waiting until they came out to feed before stalking from the top allowed us the element of surprise. Being able to shoot accurately at long range is a must.**

High Mountain Passes And Saddles

Mule deer bucks can often be found in mountain passes or natural saddles between one or more creek drainages. A saddle will usually take you from one watershed into another. Many times public trails will take advantage of these passes and saddles to make traveling from one creek drainage to another easier. However, there are many passes that see very little human traffic. Some of these have become mule deer highways into isolated basins or pockets.

I have found bucks live on or near these areas for two reasons. One, if danger comes their way, they have the chance to drop off into one of several different drainages in any direction. Many times a buck can be found perched above a pass in a scrub pine patch. This allows him the ability to watch several natural routes for any danger. Two, passes are natural corridors. Bucks can use them to move between feeding, watering and bedding areas (Fig. 8-11, pg. 117). Surprisingly if they are not threatened or bothered, a buck will live in a saddle or pass that is often frequented by humans. Some high country passes are just to busy for an old buck to call home, but don't discount an area just because it has some human activity.

In an area where I frequently hunted there is a main trail over a pass between two popular backpacking destinations. Just like clockwork, from about 10:00 a.m. until 3:00 p.m., one backpacker after another followed this trail over the top and down into the next creek drainage. They plodded along like old dude horses never veering off the trail and rarely looking around. The only thing on their minds was getting down off this high mountain pass to the basin floor before dusk.

After the sun started down and the shadows began to lengthen, several mule deer bucks would always appear out of the surrounding scrub pines. They would feed where not more than two hours earlier, humans had been traveling. For several hunting seasons after I sold my hunting camp, a friend and I would backpack into this mule deer area.

One time on this particular pass I set up my spotting scope to check out a small peak in the scrub pines just above the trail. The peak, which was still a half mile away, had areas of scrub pines on its side, providing an ideal bedding area for bucks. Suddenly, I spotted a set of antlers high above the pines. We studied the buck and estimated the rack to be about a 180 B&C gross main frame. My partner, Carl, who was new to trophy hunting, wanted to take the buck.

Just as I was returning my spotting scope into my pack, I heard what sounded like the jingle of a small bell. Looking in the direction of the sound, I spotted two backpackers heading our way on the main trail. They were both wearing shorts and as usual, had their heads down looking only at their feet and the trail directly in front of them. The man had a bandage on his right shin and another larger one on his left knee. The girl was moving along with a limp as if she had blisters on every toe.

When they stopped to chat, I asked them about the little bells attached to their backpacks. I was informed the bells were to alert any grizzlies in the area so the hikers wouldn't accidentally surprise them. Back then

©
Chris
Lacey

8-12: This is the 31-inch buck Carl took in the presence of the hikers. The drawing at the left is of the buck in his bed.

there weren't any grizzlies within 100 miles of us. With a straight face I asked if they had seen any mule deer on their trek. As I raised my binoculars to check on the position of the buck, they informed me they hadn't seen a deer since leaving Yellowstone Park two weeks ago.

Carl and I quickly said good-bye to the backpackers and started on up the trail to put a stalk on the bedded buck. We moved into position behind a large rock not 50 yards off the main trail. Carl set up using the rock for a dead rest 250 yards from the buck. Bedded within the pines the buck couldn't see us but his antlers extended above the pines, giving his position away. I gave a low whistle and the big buck got up and slowly moved out from the cover. Carl made a perfect one-shot kill (Fig. 8-12, pg. 115).

As the echo of Carl's shot died down, I heard the sound of that damn bell getting louder as they came up the trail. Suddenly a loud scream rang out, "Oh my God, they murdered a deer!" The lady hiker's voice could be heard a mile away echoing and bouncing off the canyon walls!

When the pair got up to us we were proudly taking photos of Carl's mule deer. Trying to be sociable, Carl asked if she would like her photo taken with the trophy buck. This brought on such an outburst that Carl and I couldn't keep from laughing.

Surprisingly, the girl's companion was very interested in how we hunted. He asked many questions and was concerned about how we could pack such a large animal out of the wilderness. (I think he was secretly wondering if he could use his outdoor skills to become a hunter.) We explained how we would bone out the meat and then hike 14 miles to the trailhead with our 100-pound packs. This explanation brought on more screaming about the barbaric actions of these westerners in chopping the poor animal into small pieces. Finally the couple departed, but I could hear the sound of her voice for quite some time as she loudly voiced her opinion of this great injustice.

For the past 20 years, every time I have returned to this area there has been a buck or two beneath that peak. Mule deer truly have behavior habits that can be patterned from year to year.

Tip: More than once I have watched bucks use a saddle or pass to disappear into another area. By following their route I was often able to find unknown corridors into new hunting country where trophy bucks were living. While hunting the high country, turn your spotting scope toward these saddles and passes. You'll be surprised at the bucks you'll see (Fig. 8-13, and Fig. 8-13a, pg. 118). Look above and below the saddles and timber strips that run up next to the passes. Even above the saddles on top of the world you can spot bucks making their summer home. Because they are seldom bothered by hunters these bucks have a chance to live to maturity and reach their full potential.

Tip: **8-11: High mountain passes are one of the best areas to find bucks living. They like it because if danger comes, they have the choice of dumping off into several different drainages. Carl is loaded with one of our deer that was taken on this pass between two creek drainages.**

Tip: **8-13: I have seen several very good bucks living around that pass shown by the arrows. It's one place you can always count on finding a buck.**

Tip: **8-13a: Without fail, you can find bucks living next to this pass (1.). Mule deer like having an escape route from one creek drainage into the another. Look for these types of saddles and passes that bucks use to move back and forth between drainages.**

Chapter 9

Mule Deer Behavior

Successful trophy hunters understand the importance of mule deer behavior when hunting. The more you know about this elusive creature the better your chances of taking a good buck will become.

The Strongest Sense

I am thoroughly convinced that every big game animal has one sense that is predominant over their others. For example, when whitetail deer feel excited or threatened, they put up their tail. It acts as a flag to let all other whitetail in the area know there is danger. If you've ever hunted whitetail deer, you know that along with their extremely good nose and hearing, they have the best eyesight for movement of any hooved animal. All you have to do is blink, move a finger, or even smirk, and a big whitetail buck will instantly know you are there. They have refined their sense of sight to a degree that is superior to all their other senses.

If eyesight is a whitetail's strongest sense, then hearing has to be the mule deers' greatest asset. I think mule deer have the best hearing of any animal in North America. If you watch mule deer when they first become excited, they bounce away for the first 50 yards or so before they start to run. The bounding noise is a way for them to tell other mule deer in the area there is danger upon them. It's interesting to watch the reactions of other mule deer to this bounding noise. Within a split second all the deer in the immediate area begin leaving.

I am sure mule deer can take in multiple sounds and distinguish the source of each. Humans, on the other hand, have a difficult time distinguishing between a number of sounds coming in at the same time. This ability to separate sounds helps bucks pinpoint the exact location of a particular sound. A buck will stay put and listen until he visually locates an intruder, then within a fraction of a second he formulates an escape plan that will give him the least exposure (Fig. 9-1, pg. 120).

Some of my trophy hunting buddies love to hunt mule deer on windy days because their quarry can often hear in only one direction. To a buck's acute sense of hearing, wind has much the same effect as blowing into a microphone.

Brian Suter, a tremendous trophy mule deer hunter, once walked right up on an Idaho mule deer buck. He attributes this phenomenon to the

9-1: Brian Suter was able to slip up on this buck while a hard wind was blowing. The wind interferes with the bucks' ability to hear.

hard wind that was blowing that day, the buck just didn't hear him coming.

Always remember, mule deer have a fantastic sense of eyesight and smell, but the one thing that stands out is their ability to hear. They can hear you even when you can't hear yourself!

Hunters constantly underestimate the ability of mule deer to hide and hold while a hunter walks right on by. An old buck has nerves of steel and will usually refuse to panic under hunting pressure. Younger bucks of course blow out and get shot. They will take the route of least resistance, which is often into the open. The mature deer on the other hand might just slip right by you with his head held low to the ground. They have a habit of not moving until all escape routes have been analyzed.

Time after time, whether it was driving deer for hunters or while watching other guys stalk a buck, I have seen the same scenario. The buck waits until the last minute as he considers all his options. Even if the wind is in his favor, he won't lose his head and blaze out running. Sometimes he opts to just lie there like a log and let the hunter walk right on by. This type of buck makes fools of hunters who often haven't the slightest idea a trophy buck is nearby. These are the same guys who tell me all they saw the entire fall was little 24-inch deer. They spend the whole hunt jumping from basin to basin with their guns on safety, hoping to jump a huge buck. The days of being successful with those tactics are over.

Mule deer will feed in a direction that allows them to take advantage of the thermals traveling up the slopes in the mornings and down in the evenings. They will always try to feed into the wind whenever possible. A smart mule deer hunter will use this habit to anticipate where a buck will feed and then set up an ambush. Keep in mind that bucks will sometimes have a secondary bedding spot where they lie watching their back trail for an hour or two. When they are satisfied everything is safe, they will slip into their primary bedding area for the remainder of the day.

Secret Water Holes

By the time a buck reaches seven years of age, he has learned to do much of his feeding at night, coming out after most hunters have headed back to camp. In areas that have only a one-week season, I believe a buck won't feed, instead he stays in cover until all humans have left his domain.

By eating vegetation moist with early morning dew, high country bucks can go several days without water. When they do go to water, it is often at a small north slope spring located out of sight in an isolated timber patch. The buck will drink only at night and slip back into his little sanctuary without being seen. They do, however, leave tracks and you should try to locate these special watering areas during your August scouting trips. Remember to keep a low profile as you look for buck tracks around these springs. Marking the location of them in your journal means you won't have to disturb the area again and take a chance on spooking a nervous old buck during the hunting season.

9-2: Brian hunts on foot but uses a pack horse to bring out the deer. Horses are a good alternative to lugging a big buck out on your back.

One time after spending two days in an area glassing several basins, I had spotted five small bucks but nothing big. I just knew there had to be a good buck there someplace. Finally, just before dark on the second evening, a trophy buck fed out of a patch of conifers 400 yards above the younger deer. He didn't associate with the others, but he was within 500 yards of them the whole time. This was one of those bucks who fed and watered almost entirely in the dark.

Some high country drainages have plenty of water while others may have only a small spring on the north slope. Being able to document all of these springs and feeding and bedding areas will open a door of opportunity for you. While other hunters are wandering and stumbling around the area, you will be in a pass or by a trail waiting for that big buck to come through on his way to feed or water.

Buddies

Sometimes an old buck will have a buddy he travels and lives with. It's not that he needs the company because when the rut comes, all relations are off and it's every buck for himself. The use of a less dominant buck has its advantages for the old guy. Quite obviously, two sets of eyes are better then one. Also, he will use the younger buck as a decoy if need be making him go first into the open country and again back to their bedding area. This is the most vulnerable time for him and to have a point buck is a way of keeping an edge on possible danger.

Many times I have watched the big buck go behind a patch of timber and then the younger one come out first. In fact, the older buck will strike him with his front hoof or hook him in the butt with his antlers, prodding the younger buck to go out first. Sometimes if the action gets too hot, such as when shots are fired, an old buck will turn and go the opposite direction of the younger deer. This tactic can leave you firing at the lesser buck while the monster slips down the slope and gets away. Keep in mind the older deer is not necessarily the one with the larger rack size. I have seen better scoring bucks pushed out into harm's way by an old buck with a regressed rack.

Though this is a loose relationship that sometimes lasts only a few days, it is common for an old buck to find a buddy with whom to share his bedding area.

Weather

In the high country the weather can be very severe. If you are not prepared it will easily kill you. Chances of early season snow are very good and the development of severe lightning storms is quite frequent as well. Mule deer will leave a high lookout when a severe storm rolls in. The high winds, driving rain and snow force them down to the bottom of a basin into the larger timber stands. A good rule of thumb is, two days after a big storm the bucks will start to work back up onto the high divides. Remember, they don't leave the country rather, they pull off the top and hide out in the bottoms not more then 1,000 feet below. It doesn't do you any good to stay on a 10,000-foot peak in those weather conditions.

I can remember times when lightning was cracking around me and I was the highest thing on the mountain. With wind gusts of over 60 miles per hour, tree tops were falling all around me...believe me it's no place to be. The faster you can get to safety, (the bottom of the basin), the better off you will be. Lightning is a major cause of fatalities in the outdoors.

After many years of observing deer and elk in cold country, I have concluded that when it gets 10 below zero or colder, big game animals have to leave the high country and start for the winter range. A buck can stay in snow up to his back, feeding around and under pine trees, but when the temperatures drop they have to keep a fire in their stomachs to fend off the cold. Back when we hunted into the rut you could always bet that if it got 10 below or colder the bucks would start to show up on the winter range. During cold weather, deer have to feed in the open areas several times each day on good vegetation that is high in nutritional value.

It is crucial that you as a trophy hunter, learn to identify and document the effects different weather conditions have on deer movements. Often the only way to acquire this knowledge is to develop, implement and stick to a well-structured four-year plan.

The Greatest Challenge

Observing mule deer bucks over the last 35 years I have concluded each one has his own unique personality. He will develop habits and quirks that only he will have. These individual habits make him special to hunt and the ultimate challenge for many of us. Figuring out his patterns and habits is what true trophy hunting is all about. The real joy of mule deer hunting is not the purchase of a high dollar hunt that requires only that you stake out a deer's feeding station and pull the trigger. The only challenge for that type of hunter is coming up with the money to hire the best deer spotters or trackers in that area.

My fondest memories are of the bucks that outsmarted me on their own turf and the ones I was able to take only through several years of hunting. This experience earned through hard work and uncompromising dedication is something that can't be bought.

There is no easy way to take a high mountain mule deer. At 10,000 feet you are on his ground, not in some hayfield during the rut or the migration. A special type of hunter goes after these high mountain residents, a hunter filled with dedication and motivation.

Taking a 170 buck up here is, I think, a much more rewarding trophy than a 200 B&C main frame buck off a private ranch. This is the ultimate in trophy mule deer hunting experiences. Physical and mental preparation is a must. Most hunters aren't ready for that type of commitment, which leaves the high country to hunters like us and the trophies that we so actively pursue.

My hat goes off to those of you who have taken bucks up here above the timberline. Don't be intimidated by the huge bucks being harvested in those high profile areas. Our high mountain mule deer are not for sale. So I say to you, good luck on your quest for a true high altitude trophy.

Section III

JUDGING

10-1: Being able to recognize which deer is biggest is an important part of trophy hunting. Often you will have only seconds to make a determination.

Chapter 10

Introduction to Field Judging

After years of listening to groups of trophy hunters discussing the size and shape of different types of mule deer racks, I came to realize the terms they used were often confusing and contradictory. The standard criteria changed with every hunter as they spoke of a rack's spread, mass or tine length. Some referred to a buck's size by using the net B&C score while others used the gross score. Many seemed to use an inflated outside spread (from cheater to cheater) which has no real bearing on a trophy's scoreable quality (Fig. 10-1, pg. 126).

Is there a standard every hunter can use? If you take a serious look at this section, you will discover a system that will help you describe a buck's true size to fellow hunters in terms they will immediately understand. The most important advantage is that it will help you determine trophy potential in the field.

My system, which I call Rack Bracketing, is one I came up with over 20 years ago. Growing up in one of the most productive mule deer areas in the country gave me the chance to develop this easy to use field judging system. I felt this was a necessity as the B&C system is much too complicated and complex to use in the field. It almost takes a C.P.A. just to run the calculations.

The Rack Bracketing system I have devised is easy to use and will give you a quick gross typical score in the field. You will be able to quickly estimate the largest rack among a group of comparable bucks. All it takes is a little practice such as looking at bucks in taxidermy shops, on our videos or in the field. The key is understanding what percentage of the total score is contained in each section of a mule deer's rack. Then you can quickly evaluate the various sections and come up with an estimate for the main frame score.

There are only a few simple rules and with practice you'll be able to Rack Bracket a mule deer within a few seconds. Hopefully after studying this section, bucks you take in the future will no longer suffer from that unfortunate condition known as "ground shrinkage."

Some of the topics covered are:

1. Trash Factor bucks.
2. The three typical racks and the important scoring features of each.
3. The four most important rules in determining a trophy rack.

11-1a: Would you pass up this deer? I took this buck that has a 36-inch outside spread, but just doesn't have what it takes to go book. Some of the best looking deer are this Trash Factor type.

Chapter 11

Trash Factor Buck

(The Third Type of Mule Deer)

Have you ever taken a big buck with a great main frame and several extra points? He is one heck of a buck, but when you measure him he doesn't score well in either the typical or the nontypical class. He simply falls through the cracks in the B&C record book (Fig. 11-1, pg. 130).

The Boone and Crockett measuring system plays to perfection. A typical is a standard 4-point buck that may or may not have eye guards. Any and all abnormal points are considered a deduction from the total score. The minimum typical score is 190 inches to qualify for the Boone & Crockett record book. A nontypical's score is calculated by adding the total measurement of the typical main frame plus the total of all abnormal points. The minimum nontypical score has just been lowered to 230 inches.

What about the bucks that have a big typical main frame with too many extra points to go typical and not enough to make the 230 minimum for nontypical? (Remember, to go typical all abnormal points must be measured and that total subtracted from the typical score.) There isn't category for these type of deer in the record system and they have never been truly recognized. I have always called these great trophies "Trash Factor" or "TF" bucks (Fig. 11-1a, pg. 128).

Trash Factor bucks were created by the B&C Club, but they are not recognized as a category. It happened many years ago when B&C tried to reduce the large number of entries into their record book. When they raised the minimum typical score to 195 and the nontypical minimum to 240, it left a difference of 45 points between the two categories. At the time, I felt the large increase in the minimum score was overkill. (See the trophy judging article in Issue 28 of *The Eastmans' Journal*). In 1994 the minimum for typical was lowered to 190 and as mentioned earlier, the nontypical minimum has now been lowered to 230. Although this is better on the low end, the 40-point gap still omits many bucks from the record book.

When you compare this giant 40-point spread between typical and nontypical to the spread in the whitetail category, there is quite a difference. The whitetail have a minimum of 170 typical and 190 nontypical which is a spread of only 20 points, yet the whitetail

11-1: This 36-inch deer will not go B&C because of a few non-typical points but it is still the buck of-a-lifetime. A perfect example of a Trash Factor buck.

have four times the population and four times the entries in the record book. Why then, is there only a 20-point spread between the categories? It seems to me the spread difference for mule deer is out of proportion for their population and number of entries.

In 35 years of hunting and observing mule deer, some of the biggest typical main frame bucks I've ever seen fall into the TF category. For example, looking through the B&C record book you'll notice that during the early 70s hunters took a large number of B&C heads on the Jicarilla Indian Reservation. Their typical scores often fell in the high 190s and low 200s. A few of these monsters were even bigger than the World's Record! However after the extra trash points were deducted from many of these racks, their net scores fell into the 180s, disqualifying them for entry into the record book altogether.

Most of us have seen or hunted at least one buck with a typical main frame grossing well over 190, but that carried several extra trash points. It would be absurd to think of passing up a buck like this just because his extra points would eliminate him from the B&C book (Fig. 11-2, pg. 131).

In fact, one of the biggest mule deer I've ever been associated

11-2: Brian Suter's 190-plus buck on the right won't go book because of several cheaters that have to be deducted from the typical score. Dennis' buck on the left is a good example of an even symmetrical typical buck that will go in the high 180s.

with had a heavy typical frame with webbed cheaters on each G-3 and G-4 and rectangular-shaped back points. His main frame grossed over 198. However, his 20 inches of nontypical points threw him out of the typical category. Nevertheless, I still consider him a big trophy mule deer. (The buck is in the introduction to the video Mule Deer Action Fig. 11-3, pg. 132.)

When you net out or deduct the total inches of abnormal points from a buck's typical main frame, you get a distorted picture of his true main frame size. Furthermore, when field judging this method is impractical. For these reasons it is much more desirable and realistic to give a gross instead of net typical score. It is better to explain the antler conformation by using measurements such as length of main beam, inside spread, length of back tines, gross typical score and the number of cheaters or abnormal points. Using these terms, trophy hunters are better able to explain the general size of a buck.

Extra points should not be considered a penalty. In most cases they accentuate the quality of a true trophy buck. The TF category gives credit to those exceptional bucks that don't fit into B&C's typical or nontypical categories. So the next time you're talking to a

11-3: This Teton buck from the 60s wouldn't go book but has heavy tangs and nice cheaters. Now that the minimum for non-typical has been dropped to 230, I will have him measured for the book.

fellow mule deer stalker and he mentions the gross typical score of a tremendous TF buck, you will know what he's talking about—a buck that has not enough nontypical points to make the 230 minimum but too many deductions to place him in the typical class.

Chapter 12

Rack Bracketing

Everyone has his own standard for a trophy buck. Many hunters feel a 180 buck constitutes the lower end of the trophy range, while others consider only the outside spread or mass. My personal standard is a buck packing anything over a 170 B&C gross rack. Don't let my standard sway you, come up with your own benchmark. My Rack Bracketing system will help you determine gross B&C size in seconds. Most trophy hunters aren't interested in the net B&C score, but rather what the rack will gross without deductions.

Rack Bracketing is easy to learn and will help you quickly determine a buck's gross rack size in the field. In order to use it, you need to understand several points. First, this system is not used to calculate a precise net B&C score. Instead, it gives you a benchmark for determining a buck's general gross main frame score. You can also use it to determine which mule deer in a group of bucks has the best scoring rack. With practice, you'll be able to quickly categorize a buck into one of four main frame configurations: 150 gross, 170 gross, 180 gross, and super bucks over 190 gross typical score. You will be able to calculate the gross main frame score within eight B&C points. This system may also be used on blacktail deer.

Actually, there are only three basic types of typical rack configurations. Even nontypical bucks will carry one of these three types of typical main frames. To accurately evaluate a buck, you first need to know which type of rack he is packing.

1. The first is a buck with good fronts and bad backs. He has long main beams and a good inside spread. The inside spread is the only spread that counts in scoring. It's great to have a 30-inch outside spread but it's not a determining factor when scoring a buck. The G-4s on this type of buck are almost as high as his back tines, however his G-3s branch high off the G-2s. Remember, 65 percent of a buck's total score comes from his fronts (Fig. 12-1, pg. 136).

2. The second type of buck has good back tines and short fronts which means his main beams and G-4 are both short, having what are commonly called "crab claw" fronts. When the minimum typical score was at 195, these bucks would generally not go in. However, with the minimum

Typical Main Frame

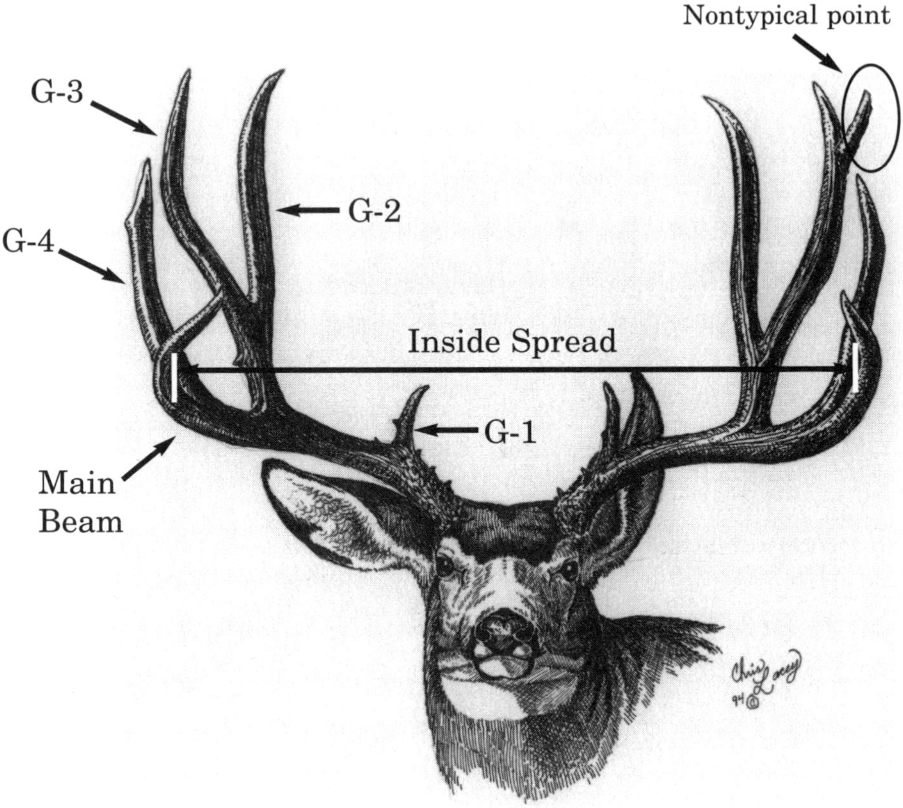

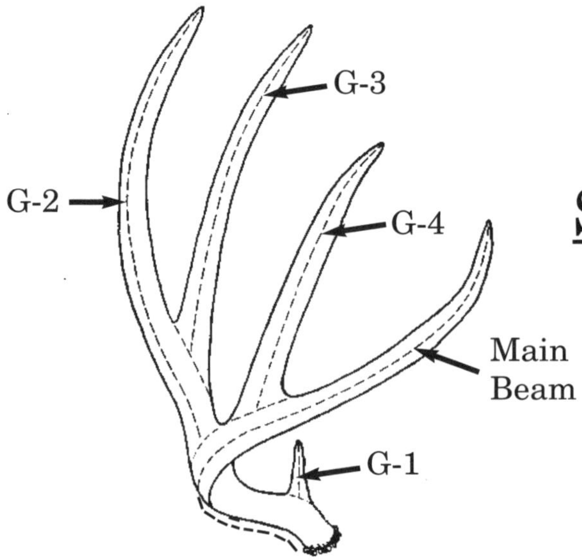

Side View

Rack Bracketing

Note: **12-1: This buck has good fronts but his back tangs (G-2, see pg. 134) are short. Notice his wide rack size, with cheaters it is over 34 inches outside.**

now at 190, some of these types will now go book (Fig. 12-2, pg. 137).

3. The third type will have both good front tines and good back tines. He is very symmetrical and well-rounded. This deer is the most difficult to judge because he doesn't have any outstanding features. Even an experienced hunter may misjudge this type of rack.

In future chapters we will discuss the implications each rack form has on the gross typical score. Becoming familiar with the three typical rack conformations is very important to Rack Bracketing and field judging in general.

Rules for Rack Bracketing

1. Good fronts make up for bad backs, 65 percent of the total score comes from the fronts.
2. Inside spread can't exceed the length of the main beam.
3. If the rack is wider than it is high…move on.
4. Mass is only 18 percent of the total score.

To practice what you have learned in this section, I suggest using our videos, Mule Deer Stalker I and Mule Deer Stalker II. They will give you

Note: **12-2: This buck has good backs but crab-claw fronts. Remember 65 percent of the total B&C score comes from the front. That is the main beam, inside spread, and G-4s. This is a 170 class buck.**

in-depth information on Rack Bracketing and you'll see many different rack configurations. Also practice on mounted bucks in sporting goods stores, taxidermy shops or trophies your friends have hanging on their walls. The best way to sharpen your skills, however, is to study bucks in the field.

As you practice separating racks into one of the three size categories, it will soon become second nature to categorize every rack you lay your eyes on. This is the first step in quickly identifying a buck's true rack size.

Note: **12-5: The buck in the back is a strong 190 deer. He has a 30-inch outside main frame. Good fronts and back tangs that branch low are what makes this deer. The front buck is a low 180 with good back tangs that bow in at the top, but his main beams are a little short. The G-4s are short and he also loses at least six inches of score because of no eye guards. Also, he has only a 19-inch inside spread.**

12-5a: This 190-plus mule deer has good backs but his G-4 and main beams are short (refer to pg. 134). Even at that this buck scores well over 190 B&C.

12-3: A good example of an even symmetrical 180 buck. Notice his good backs and main beams that are 26 inches long. The G-4s are 10 inches long, this is a good trophy deer.

12-4: The Hornbeck brothers picked up this buck's left antler one winter, it scored 83 4/8. Mirror the other side and give him a 24-inch inside spread and you have a 190 deer. Big backs and respectable fronts make this good buck go into that super 190-plus class.

Chapter 13

Spread

"Inside spread cannot exceed the length of main beam."

Many hunters put too much emphasis on spread. As I travel around the country doing my shows and seminars, I hear many hunters refer to their trophies in terms of spread only. Some say they have turned down mulies in the 28- to 29-inch class looking for that magical 30-inch spread. Using spread as their only criteria with no regard for point or main beam length, I've always wondered how many of these hunters passed up 190-class bucks because they had only a 28-inch spread.

A similar scenario is the hunter who says he has a 32-inch mule deer mounted on the wall. Upon further investigation, his buck really has a 26-inch main frame spread with a 3-inch cheater off the back tines on both sides. It is a nice buck, but not a true 30-inch rack.

I've measured many bucks over the years and found a true 30-inch outside main frame is rare. In my opinion, spread is not the only benchmark for a quality buck.

Mule deer hunters who are familiar with the B&C scoring system know spread isn't all it's cracked up to be. It counts for only a small portion of the total measurement. The Boone and Crockett scoring system counts only the inside spread as one of the many calculations for the final net total score. Their book says the inside spread cannot exceed the length of the main beam. In other words, if the inside spread is wider than the length of the main beam, you can only add the length of the main beam as your spread on the score sheet. In the record book, you won't see many bucks with a true 30-inch inside spread (Fig. 13-1, pg. 142).

More important than outside spread is a combination of main beam length, length of all typical points and the inside spread. If you are fortunate enough to take a buck with some additional points, they are an added bonus. The most desirable type of buck seems to be one with mass and some good kickers coming off the back tines. Although these kickers are deductions from the net score they are my personal favorite.

Keith Dana, who is an official B&C scorer and avid mule deer hunter, has a saying that makes sense: "If the buck is wider than he is high, keep looking." In other words, if he doesn't have good tine length and his spread is greater than the length of his main beam, then he's just a buck.

Being able to determine the width of a buck's rack is an art. A helpful

13-1: Popeye has an inside spread of over 30 inches and an outside spread of over 40. This Wyoming buck's main frame gross scores over 220 B&C.

pointer in field judging a buck's spread is that most bucks have a 22-inch spread ear-tip to ear-tip. However, I've seen some bucks with foreheads two inches wider than normal. Therefore, you may have to compensate for this additional width in your spread estimate.

In the early 70s when I first hunted Colorado, they had deer running everywhere. If you had the proper tags, you could take several bucks during the season. I had passed up several bucks in what I judged to be the 28-inch spread class. I felt they were good deer gross-scoring in the 180s, but not that super 190 main frame I was looking for. After several days of hard hunting Jeff Warren, my hunting partner, chose to take one of the 28-inch bucks we had passed up earlier in the hunt.

After packing the buck back to camp, I put the tape across his rack from outside to outside. To my surprises the buck had a whopping 30 1/2-inch outside main frame! His main beams were 26 inches long and his inside spread was 25 inches pushing him up to a 190-class super buck. I scratched my head in disbelief, "How could I be that far off?" I measured again. Sure enough, he was 30 1/2. About that time I noticed his head was as wide as a mule's. As I stretched the tape from ear-tip to ear-tip, it was almost 25 inches across. His was not your average 22-inch ear-tip to ear-tip deer head.

Gordon Eastman with the number two B&C typical that came from the Jackson Hole country has only a 27-inch spread, but look at those long tangs and main beams.

One way of determining if a buck has an oversized head is to look at his forehead width compared to the other bucks he is running with. However, the best way is to get a front view and determine if he looks exceptionally wide. If he has a big, wide Roman nose, it is a clue that he has an unusually wide head. Some areas produce wide-headed deer. However, one of these may be found in any region or deer herd. A 25-inch inside spread can make a big difference when rack bracketing mule deer in the field. Adding three inches or more to the bottom net score of the buck can make all the difference in the world.

When it comes to spread, a super buck doesn't have to be 30-inches wide. Many bucks with a 28-inch outside main frame spread will gross 190 or better. I often think of all the B&C racks thrown in sheds or the back yard from the 60s because they weren't that magical 30 inches wide. Like most guys, I like to see a true 30-inch main frame with antlers that go straight out past the ears and turn up (Fig. 13-2, pg. 144; Fig. 13-3, pg. 145; Fig. 13-5, pg. 146; Fig. 13-6, pg. 146; .Fig. 13-4, pg. 148). Remember, when field judging a buck the spread is only as good as the length of the main beam. A buck with long tines will always score better than one with a wide spread.

Another problem the hunter has to deal with when it comes to judging spread is "ground shrinkage." Sometimes, after a hunter has taken a buck, he discovers the rack is suddenly half the size he thought it was. What's the deal? When a buck walks away from you, he pinches his ears back so he can rotate them and listen to your movements as he leaves. When he does this, more blue sky shows between his ears and rack making the antlers seem twice is wide.

However when a buck stands at attention and looks straight at you, you can use his ears to determine the width of the inside and outside spread. If the outside of the main beam is wider than the ear tips, it is a good indication the buck has a 24-inch or better inside spread. On the other hand, if his ear tips are sticking out past the main beams there is a good chance his inside spread is under 23 inches (Fig. 13-7 and Fig 13-8, pg. 147).

You can practice these techniques by looking at every mounted buck you see. Use the ears for a measuring stick and practice judging the

13-2: This buck taken near Big Piney, Wyoming, has a 32-inch outside spread and a 26-inch inside spread. Even though it won't make the 190 B&C minimum this buck's wide rack is appealing to most hunters.

length of the main beam and inside spread. It won't be long before you can easily estimate a buck's inside spread and main beam length. The secret to becoming a good judge of spread is to carry a tape measure and put it on every buck's spread you come across. After a few times of doing this you will be able to look at the buck and give a close estimate of spread width.

13-3: My father, Gordon Eastman, with a deer he took in the late 60s with an outside spread of 32 inches. There is a lot of air between the ears and the outside edge of the rack. It scored 189 1/8 B&C, but back then we didn't care much about scoring systems.

Tip: **13-5: This buck has only a 29-inch outside spread but will score 190 B&C. Notice his 5 1/2-inch eye guards. However, he has a six-inch drop tine behind his ear on the left side keeping him out of the record book.**

Note: **13-6: Keith Palmer with his 190 B&C record book deer. This buck proves you don't need a 30-inch plus buck to have a big deer, the length of the tangs give it its high score.**

Which buck is bigger?

Note: **13-7: How many times have you seen a buck looking over 30 inches wide as he ran away with his ears pinched back listening to you.**

Photo by author

Note: **13-8: Now look at the same buck (Fig. 13-7) from the front and you'll notice he is only about 27 inches wide. They always look bigger running away.**

Photo by author

Note: **13-8a: This is the same buck again. Never judge a buck from only the side view of his rack. There is no reference to length of tines, main beam or inside spread.**

Photo by author

Answer: *These are all of the same buck. The photos were all taken on the winter range within 30 minutes.*

13-4: My brother, Rod, and I work on one of my high mountain mule deer. It has a 30-inch main frame and a 32-inch outside cheater spread, but only scored in the high 170s. To most trophy hunters, 30 inches is the magic number.

Chapter 14

Good Fronts Make Up For Bad Backs

Some hunters think good back tines are the most important feature in making a buck's rack score well. The truth of the matter is, good fronts always make the buck score higher. I learned this fact during a perilous experience as a teenager in Jackson Hole, Wyoming, during the 1960s.

I was hunting with my father, Gordon Eastman, during a late season hunt that ran through the end of December. I had spotted a buck across the Snake River Canyon on a snowy weekend. It was near the end of the season with frigid 10 below zero temperatures. After scoping him out, it was evident his G-3 branched very high on the G-2. He was far from being the well-rounded, symmetrical buck I was always looking for. However, he did have good main beams with high G-4s and a strong inside spread.

Finally on December 31, the last day of the season, the weather broke. (That is if you consider clear skies, 35 degrees below zero with a 15 mile per hour wind and waist-deep snow a break!)

Dad said, "It's time to go for it, kid!"

The only way to reach the buck was to row our rubber raft across the slush-filled Snake River. Ice creates some serious problems on a river the size and speed of the Snake. The bottom of the rubber boat would ride on top of several hundred pounds of frozen slush-ice, making it very difficult to row across to the other side. As we inched toward the opposite shore, the current continued to push us downstream. Finally making it to the other side, Dad had to row backward to keep the boat from slamming into the opposite bank while I chopped out the sharp ice with the spare oar to make a safe landing area for the boat. If we weren't careful, the knife-sharp edge of ice on the bank would slice through our boat, leaving us stranded on the opposite shore miles from any shelter.

The buck was located on a south sagebrush slope accompanied by about a dozen does. After landing the boat safely, we circled around to come in well above the buck. Taking turns breaking trail through the waist-deep snow, we slowly worked our way around the north timbered side of the ridge. We used the timber as cover all the way, even though deeper snow on the north side of the ridge made travel much more difficult.

The deep snow forced use to rest often, but with patience we were

14-2: Using a rubber raft, Dad and I floated across the Snake River in 35 below zero weather to hunt mule deer for several seasons in the 60s.

able to work within 250 yards of the buck and his does. Because the old buck was rutting he didn't see us, but the does picked up on our movements and started to get nervous. Dad instructed me to take a dead rest through the fork of a small pine tree. I placed the crosshairs in the middle of the buck's shoulder and slowly squeezed the trigger of my 7mm magnum. The muzzle blast knocked down the snow from the overhanging branches, completely covering my rifle and me. Luckily the shot was well placed and the smart old buck went down, because with my face, eyes and scope full of snow, I would never have had another chance. The snow falling down my neck and into my ears chilled me until I warmed up by walking over to the buck.

It was getting dark by the time we dragged the buck back to the river and loaded it into the rubber raft. I can still hear the constant roar of that ice-filled river. It was now pitch dark making me wonder if the buck was worth the danger we were now facing. To cross the river and hit a suitable landing spot on the opposite side, we had to float downstream through a dangerous series of dump-off rapids. A dump-off is formed when all the water in that section of the river funnels into a single chan-

Chris
© Lacey
1997

14-3: This trip got a little western before it was over. If we had capsized, we would have almost surely died in the severe cold. I would go to any lengths to get a good mule deer back then.

nel forming a steep chute with three-foot high rapids and white caps.

As I looked at the sides of the raft, I could see the water was within only a few inches of coming over the side boards. With two men and a big-bodied deer in the small craft, I knew one mistake would pitch us into the slushy ice water. The air temperature had to be 30 below…no time to take a swim.

Dad needed to maneuver into the dump-off at just the right angle or the raft would surely flip upside down. So with a flashlight in hand, I leaned out over the front of the raft trying to shine as much light as possible on the approaching drop. Dad expertly rowed us into position and we hit the chute perfectly. The current grabbed us and we shot down through the narrows with ease. There was no time to rest, however, as the splashing water continued to freeze on the rowing frame making the boat even heavier and harder to row. When I glanced at the buck lashed on the back seat, his antlers were covered with six-inch icicles, making him look like a big trash-factor buck.

Fortunately for us, the river current began to push us toward the opposite shore and before long we landed safely. We were cold and wet,

14-4: This is the buck I took after floating across the Snake River pg. 151). It has been hanging in a bar in Jackson for the last 35 years. When I killed this buck, it qualified for the book because of the good fronts, main beams, G-4s and inside spread. Also notice the 4-inch eye guards.

but thankful to be alive.

In the early 60s, Dad was one of the pioneers in floating fisherman on both the Green and Snake Rivers. Although owning and using rubber rafts was relatively new at that time, Dad was well-versed in the skill. We crossed the river during the late hunting season several more times over the next few years under much the same conditions. In fact, in the video Rocky Mountain Safari Deer, there is a segment on this type of adventure.

Hunting with Dad was always a little western. He wouldn't hesitate go the extra mile to look over the next ridge. He hunted areas that most hunters found too difficult, but it always paid off. We saw some huge bucks in those years. These experiences taught me how to move around in country lacking trails and hunt the rough high areas where there wasn't much traffic.

In those days hunting was not only a physical challenge, but could be very dangerous as well. The extremes we went to for a trophy buck were an important part of the game. Now, it seems if you have the money you can put yourself in a rancher's alfalfa field looking at bucks that live the

14-1: Because of the good fronts, this 27-inch buck will gross in the high 170s.

good life. However, if you are looking for the physical and mental challenge of hunting a wary old buck, that challenge can still be found on the public lands of the high country.

Later that winter, I had the buck officially measured. To my surprise, with his 25-inch main beams and 24-inch inside spread, he went 186 B&C. At that time, 185 was minimum for typical (Fig. 14-4, pg. 153).

After that, I realized good fronts make a trophy buck because 65 percent of his total score comes from his fronts. This is true for two reasons. First, a good main beam can be as much as 25 to 27 inches long which more than makes up for the length of any back tine. Second, the inside spread measurement adds to the score especially if the inside spread is over 24 inches.

Since the inside spread cannot exceed the length of the main beam, a bow-shaped main beam gives you the best of two worlds…the longest main beam measurement and the greatest possible inside spread measurement. The exception to this rule is the mulie with high, vertical main beams that result in a narrow inside spread (Fig. 17-2, pg 167).

You can test this for yourself by holding your arms up over your head as if they were antlers. Your arms are about 30 inches long. When you hold them straight up, the distance in between your arms represents about an 18-inch inside spread. However when you allow your arms to go more horizontal, the inside spread becomes much greater yet your arms represent the same 30-inch length. Because of the wider inside spread, it results in a high-scoring buck (Fig. 13-1, pg 142).

Determining the length of the main beams isn't hard when you compare them to the buck's ears. A normal buck will have a 10-inch ear length. If you can imagine placing one ear length after the other end to end up the main beam, you can come very close to estimating actual length. A good main beam is 2 1/2 ear lengths, which is over 25 inches. Bucks with short 18- to 22-inch main beams will have two or less ear lengths. Try it yourself by using a mounted deer or some of the bucks in our videos. With a little practice, you can soon become proficient at this skill.

After looking at the main beam, the next point to consider is the G-4. This is the front point that protrudes from the main beam. This one tine can propel a 160 buck into the 170 class. Let's say a deer has good 16-inch back tines that fork low and short main beams about 22 inches long. He will most likely fall into the 170 typical class. However, if you took the same buck and gave him a 25-inch main beam, a 24-inch inside spread, and a long G-4, he will be pushing the 180 class. Twelve to 16-inch G-4s will help boost the total score.

To jump up to the super 190-plus buck, the fronts need to have 26- to 28-inch main beams, G-4s almost as long as the back tines, well-balanced back tines that branch low with the G-2 at least 18 inches long, and an inside spread of at least 25 inches.

Tip: Remember, the first thing you look for in field judging is good main beams and high G-4s. Then how wide is the inside spread? Next determine if the back tines (G-2) are long with good low forks (G-3), or short and branch high? In your mind, you can now begin to calculate the gross score.

If you measure a lot of mule deer, you'll find that a buck with good back tines and short fronts will have a tough time going book. (However, now that the typical minimum has been lowered to 190 net, some of these high tined, short main beam racks will go book.) On the other hand, a buck with good fronts and average back forks will often go B&C. The front part of his rack: the main beam lengths, inside spread width, and length of G-4s make up 65 percent of the buck's total score. I've discovered that 80 percent of all trophy mule deer fall into two rack categories; good backs with small fronts or good fronts with high-branching back tines. Then there are the 20 percent that have good main beams, high G-4s, 25-inch plus inside spread, and good back tines. These big deer fall into the category I call "super symmetrical bucks."

If you see two big mulies standing side-by-side and the first one has great back tines while the second has good main beams with G-4s close to the same height as his back tines, the second one is almost always the better trophy. Also if two bucks are staring at you and both have good backs but one has longer main beams, he will definitely be the better scoring deer.

The hardest bucks to judge are those with even, boxy racks. Because all the tines are the same length and they have no outstanding features like an extra wide spread or maybe high back tines, hunters have a difficult time determining their score. The secret to evaluating this type of deer is to compare his overall rack size to his ear-to-ear width. These bucks need to have an inside spread of about two inches past the ears, low branching back tines and G-4s that are at least 12 inches long. With these features, you're looking at a solid 170 rack. Some of the best scoring, symmetrical, boxy bucks are underestimated by even experienced trophy hunters. These bucks just don't look that impressive because none of their features stand out. They just appear to be of average size.

The World's Record typical, the Burris Buck, is one of those symmetrical average looking deer. However if you put the tape on his tines you will find he is extremely impressive. With long main beams and a 27-inch plus inside spread the buck is a true number one head.

14-05a Kyle Balzly's buck has both good fronts and good backs and his main typical frame grosses well over 200 B&C.

14-6: Even though this buck I'm holding is narrow, he has good 25-inch main beams and excellent back tines. Without that dropper, he would have made the book.

15-5: A perfect example of a buck that has developed giant backs and short fronts.

Chapter 15

Good Back Tines

When Boone and Crockett lowered the minimums for typical mule deer from 195 to 190, it allowed some of those bucks with short main beams but good back tines to qualify for the record book. Before the change it was almost impossible for a buck with good backs and weak fronts to go B&C. The reason is 65 percent of the total score comes from the front part of the rack that includes the inside spread, main beam length and the G-4.

In order for a buck with weak fronts (short main beams and G-4) to make book you have to find one with no nontypical points as deductions. He must also have back tangs that measure at least 19 inches long with low forking G-3s. Some mule deer areas such as those around Jackson Hole, Wyoming, have an antler gene pool that produces those racks with good backs but short main beams (commonly called crab pincher fronts).

Finding a mule deer buck that has both good fronts, (main beam, inside spread and G-4's), and good back tines can be very difficult. Over the years I have seen so many of those high back tined bucks that fall way short on the main beams and G-4s. Remember good fronts will make up for bad backs but it's almost impossible to find a buck that goes book with only good backs.

Back tines (G-2, G-3) make up the second section of the rack you should evaluate, making sure the G-3 branches low off the G-2. When a buck is running away the back tines are the first portion of the rack you notice and good backs will stick out like a sore thumb.

Many years ago when I was in my teens I had been hunting late in the year around Jackson Hole. This was in December and the deer had moved down onto their historical wintering range.

I located a buck that at the time I thought was a monster. Twice I jumped him out of his bed only to watch him in bound into the timber and disappear. Dad had just come back from one of his lecture tours so I had told him about the buck and he agreed to give me a hand. Early the next afternoon we went up into the drainage where the buck was wintering.

After reaching the general area, we split up to hunt. I went into the canyon where I had last seen the buck while Dad took the next canyon up the creek. Just as the sun was going down, I heard one shot from the canyon where my father was hunting. Making my way over to his location, I found Dad dragging the buck. He had waited until the deer came

15-1: One of my Dad's big bucks. Back then we didn't worry about the score, we just knew he was a large deer. Even with his short fronts, he's still a big trophy mule deer.

out that evening to feed and stalked within 300 yards. By using this tactic rather than jumping the buck as I had been doing, he was able to make the kill.

The buck was very impressive with exceptional back tines although short in the fronts. So the second most important part of a mule deer's rack are his back tines. With the minimum now lowered to 190, a buck with good backs and short fronts can still net out high enough to make book.

15-4: Here I rough score a buck taken by a fellow hunter on an early high mountain hunt in the Jackson Hole, Wyoming area.

15-3: Dennis Suter on the left has a high back-tanged buck that wouldn’t go book at the time it was taken due to the short main beams. Now he will get into the 190 B&C minimum. It's still a mule deer of-a-lifetime. His brother Brian's nontypical on the right also qualifies for B&C, scoring 240 with a 40-inch outside spread.

15-2: These days a buck like this with good backs will make the book whereas a few years ago he wouldn't when the minimum was 195.

Chapter 16

Eye Guards

The small point just above the antler burr is called the G-1 or eye guard. Typically they're not very long yet their importance is often overlooked when field judging. A five-inch eye guard will propel a high 170 buck into the next rack bracketing classification of 180. On the downside, a 180 buck without eye guards could be thrown down into the 170 class.

Some areas tend to produce bucks with no eye guards while other areas grow better then average G-1s. An average mulie rack will have three-inch eye guards, but on some racks they can measure as long as five to six inches. When this happens, it can quickly add six points to the bottom line of a gross typical score. A 186 main frame deer with four more inches of eye guard suddenly becomes a 190 plus super buck. So pay close attention to these little points and make them the third section of the rack you study when bracketing a buck's antlers.

16-1: The third thing to look at on a buck is the eye guards.

Tip: **16-2: This Jackson Hole buck has 5 1/2-inch eye guards that add to the main frame score. With his long cheaters the buck's outside spread was over 30 inches.**

Tip: **16-3: With no eye guards, this buck loses three inches on each side taking a potential 162 B&C buck down to a 150. Eye guards are important, and in some cases will make the difference between a great scoring buck or just a good deer.**

Chapter 17

Mass

Back when I was outfitting for trophy mule deer, a gentleman booked a special 14-day solo trophy hunt. He had hunted every hot spot from the Jicarilla Indian Reservation to the Ruby Mountains of Nevada. Although he had spent thousands of dollars in his quest for a B&C mulie, he always seemed to be in the right place at the wrong time and had never connected with a top head.

I scouted my area late that summer when the reds were on and located what I believed to be a surefire B&C buck. Actually, one of my hunters had missed this buck during a September hunt the year before. Just like clockwork he came back to the same summering area. His main beams were about 27 inches long with an inside spread of 24 inches and tines in the back that forked low. The G2s had to be 18 inches long if they were an inch. The only thing that might keep him out of the book was an extra five-inch point coming off his left G-2. This buck-of-a-lifetime would surely gross over 195 B&C! I named him the Spear Point Peak buck because he summered on a peak that was shaped like a spear point.

With no trails into the remote basin, I felt confident no one else would slip in on opening day and spook him out. However my biggest problem would be getting the hunter to the peak before morning light touched the basin. The hunter wasn't acclimated to the 11,000 foot altitude; furthermore he was in poor physical shape. Climbing at that altitude can take a lot out of a hunter especially when traveling in the dark on narrow, steep deer trails.

Early on opening morning while the stars were still bright, we left spike camp and inched our way through several rock slides and along knife ridges to the isolated peak. Due to the extremely difficult terrain, we arrived a bit late after the sun had begun to highlight the surrounding peaks. I left the hunter resting on the back side while I low crawled to the edge to scope out the peak. Being careful not to silhouette myself against the morning sky, I started glassing the steep, rocky ribbon benches that made up the peak. It didn't take long to spot a long-tanged buck quartering away at 200 yards. He was feeding quickly toward his bedding area in a timber strip.

I urgently motioned for the hunter to join me. With a flat boulder as a dead rest, I instructed him to hold right on behind the shoulder. There was no time for the hunter to study the antlers, he would just have to take my word for the buck's size.

By then the buck had stopped eating but continued moving toward the

17-1: The hunter can't get his hand around the beams on this heavy old buck taken in western Wyoming. A heavier rack you won't find anywhere. Even though it won't go book, it is very near the top on my personal list of favorites.

17-3: Using a tape to get a rough score is ok, but it is best to take it to a measurer. Here I rough measure the buck's gross typical score.

17-2: This buck was killed in my outfitting area. At the time it wouldn't go book because of its long cheaters, but is now eligible with its 192 net B&C score. The Boone and Crockett measurer told me it was the heaviest typical he had ever weighed on the scales. Mass is impressive and a desirable trait in antler confirmation.

trees. My hunter had just enough time for one bear-down shot. Instead, he scoped out the antlers then turned to me and exclaimed the buck just wasn't heavy enough to go book. I stared in disbelief as the huge deer disappeared into the timber. Later that morning, I sat the hunter down on a grassy alpine slope and explained what it takes to make a B&C buck.

Every year I talk to many avid hunters who pass up good, long-tined bucks looking for webbed points and massive racks. Personally, I too like to hunt for heavy racks even if it means passing up a high tined buck. I've always considered mass to be an added bonus in antler appeal, but it is often over-emphasized when determining the scoring quality of a trophy mule deer.

You must keep in mind that mass is only 18 percent of the total score. When scoring antlers using the Boone and Crockett system, circumference measurements are taken at the smallest point of each of the four designated positions. Usually the smallest point on a heavy rack is only slightly larger then on an average-weight rack. Think about that! The four smallest circumference measurements of a heavy rack will generally add only four to six points to each side of the main frame score. So in order for a light-racked buck to make up for lack of mass, he only needs one to two additional inches of length on all four of his tines.

When you're looking at a buck that has long tines but doesn't seem very heavy, don't write him off. He may score higher than you think. Also, mass has a way of distorting tine length by as much as 15 percent. Heavy back tines will often appear to be shorter than they really are. So when scoping out and Rack Bracketing a heavy buck, be sure to take that fact into consideration. Remember, spread, mass, number of points and length of tines all make each buck unique. Although a heavy-horned buck is more desirable to many of us, mass is not a major determining factor when estimating B&C gross score or Rack Bracketing.

The following year I once again located the Spear Point Peak buck. His rack size was the same but he had lost his good back tangs and the G-4s were only four inches long. A buck probably has only one or two years when he will produce a B&C rack, then he either trashes out or his main frame will regress.

If you're a hunter who prefers massive antlers, it will help to know that certain areas consistently produce these types of racks. Many people think it's due to the minerals, others think it's purely genetic. Probably a combination of both is closer to the truth.

Even in good areas, bucks have to put on enough age to allow the pedestals to grow large enough to support heavy-based antlers. When a buck is five years old or older, he usually begins to get heavier and develop extra points. Then as he draws close to the end of his life, his antlers will regress to short, heavy points. In the video Mule Deer Stalker II, you'll see a six year-old buck with a 204 main frame that regresses to a short, stubby rack by the time he is 11 years old.

Some areas that produce heavy antlers are in northern Arizona, southern Utah and in parts of southern Colorado where good game management is practiced. In past years some areas of western Wyoming and southeastern Idaho have also produced this desirable trait. It is possible, however, to find a heavy deer in just about any terrain.

Note: In the West, mass is only one of the many traits hunters look for in a trophy mule deer. However in some European countries, it is the only factor for measuring the quality of a rack. England uses the water displacement method to determining the size of antlers. They fill a tub with a specific amount of water, set the antlers in it and record the amount of water that is displaced.

Another method requires the antlers weigh 28 kilos or more to be consider a top head. That is their only criteria. Neither system takes into consideration tine length or antler conformation. I think it would add an interesting dimension to our scoring system to know the weight of record book antlers.

Section IV

Trophy Bucks

"Champ"

(Jack Hone with Champ's antlers.)

Jack Hone has been watching this buck for three years. Champ is a big nontypical that lives not in the high country, but instead makes his home in the desert of southern Wyoming. This desert is located in a general hunting area. With hundreds of hunters moving through his home range you would think someone would have found this buck. However Champ is so allusive, only two guys have photos of him. Unfortunately because of the distance at which the photos were taken, they are not good enough to print.

Jack has found two years of Champ's antlers and in 95-96 the buck's nontypical score was 228 with a 197 main frame. Each of the last two years Champ has broken off his large horizontal cheater on the passenger side. If he were to hold on to that eight-inch point, his outside spread would be over 42 inches. (Maybe next year!) He is a young buck (only about five years old), and I think he has a lot of growing to do in the future.

Chapter 18

Trophy Bucks

Big Bucks And Antler Growth

To me one of the most fascinating things about mule deer is their antler growth from year to year. Not much in the way of studies have been done on this subject, however, over the years I have found guys who have collected the shed antlers of large trophy deer. In this section we will look at some of Wyoming's biggest mule deer and their antler progression through the years.

I believe there are three unique aspects of these deer. One, they are found on public land. Two, all three bucks were hunted by residents and nonresidents alike on public land. Third is the photo record and several years of their antlers. Knowing the history of these bucks helps hunters understand antler growth on big deer. Make no mistake, the road to good trophy deer comes with limited numbers of hunters and the availability of good wintering areas. When these two elements are available, you can produce those super bucks we all like to see.

You need to remember that regional genetic make up will influence antler traits and conformation. For example, in the Jackson Hole, Wyoming area bucks generally have good back tines and short main beams. If you can find one with good 26-inch main beams, he will push 180 gross.

In southern Utah and northern Arizona, bucks will typically have heavy, massive antlers with a nontypical Trash Factor influence. Because of the trash points, these bucks often lack the score to go book typical but are still huge gross mainframe typical trophies. Most hunters put too much emphasis on genetics and not enough on good management. I believe there are many potentially good mule deer areas if they were managed properly.

Five Years Of The Hornbeck Buck

Photos by John and Kirby Hornbeck

This series of photos by John and Kirby Hornbeck provide us with a rare look at the antler development of a trophy mule deer. The Hornbecks filmed this big Wyoming nontypical on the winter range each year from 1989-94. The buck had unique "signature points" on the left G-4 and on the right G-3 and G-4.

In 1992, the buck developed double eye-guards but in 1993 he regressed somewhat due to a severe winter. The year after that was mild, however, and the huge antlers came back as big as ever.

You'll note in '94, he still had the double eye guards plus a 40-inch outside spread. With good fronts, 27-inch main beams, 14-inch plus G-4s, a 24-inch spread plus all his extra points, he will qualify for the record book.

Since the old buck lives in an area that is open to hunting, he must have a great hiding place to have survived all of these years. John is one of the few hunters to have had a chance at this deer. Several years ago, he drew a late season permit for the area and had the buck spotted, but was unable to connect when a dense fog rolled in.

The Eastman video Mule Deer Stalker II features John Hornbeck's great winter range footage of this huge buck up close and personal.

1989

1990

1992

1993

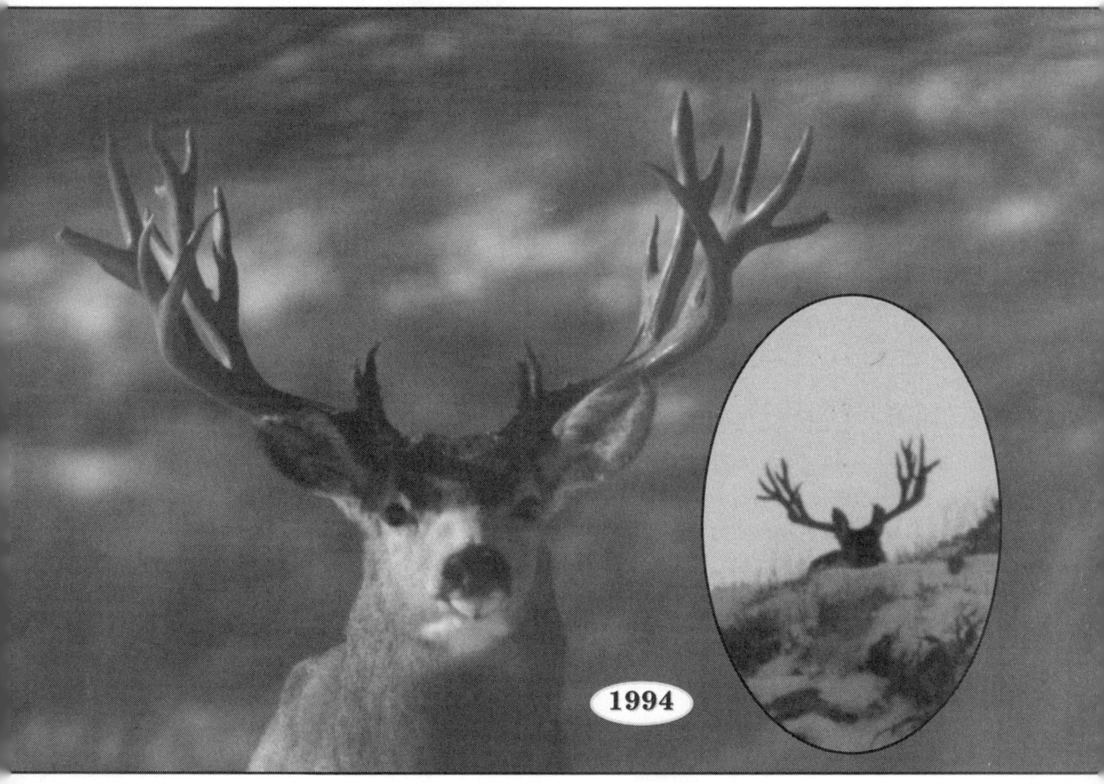
1994

Photo by Rod Hart

Release Of Locked Bucks

There have been many locked-up whitetail bucks found, but it is much more rare to find mule deer in this predicament. To find mule deer bucks that are still alive and locked is rare indeed. Add the ability to film and document this event and you have something that everyone would like to witness. The staff of *The Eastmans' Journal* was very fortunate to record such an event during the 1995 Wyoming hunting season.

Journal editor, Rod Hart's brother, Roger, came upon these locked bucks while hunting during a special late deer season. Roger called *The Journal* and we all rushed out to see if we could help.

Thanks to Rod Hart's expert roping ability, we were able to immobilize the live buck, saw off one of his antlers and set him free. Things got real western as I was almost gored several times in addition to nearly being kicked in the head!

In Mule Deer Stalker II you can see the whole ordeal on video. I know of no other footage like this and the still photos in this book show how dramatic the event was. If he hadn't been set free, the live buck would have died a terrible death as coyotes would have literally eaten him alive.

Several weeks later we found the one-horned buck. He was doing all right but wasn't chasing does anymore! He probably figured it wasn't worth the risk of losing his life.

Photo by Author

Photo by Rod Hart

After roping the buck, we were able to immobilize him and saw his antlers free. The video Mule Deer Stalker II shows the whole ordeal of releasing the locked-up buck. Photos on these two pages by Mike and Guy Eastman

“Popeye”

Eddie Boe, an avid shed collector and photographer who lives in southwestern Wyoming, has been following the winter range activities of a giant nontypical buck. In addition to recovering several sets of the buck's sheds, Eddie has been able to film and photograph him at very close range. Mule deer observers in this part of the state have dubbed the massive buck “Popeye,” because your eyes pop out when you see him!

Popeye's main beams go almost straight out. He has an inside spread of over 28 inches, with a main frame outside spread of 37 1/2 to 40 inches, depending on the year. His antler configuration is such that the rack looks just as wide from the front as from the back. I believe his 1996-97 year has a 40-inch outside main frame spread.

Larger bucks have been filmed in other states, but there are three things that make this buck so special. One, he lives on public land and during the fall is hunted in a general area in Wyoming. Two, staying out of harm's way for almost a decade, this buck migrates 70 air miles between summer and winter ranges. (Popeye has been coming to the same public land wintering grounds for the past seven years.) Third is the documentation of his antler growth through my videos and *The Eastmans' Journal* hunting magazine.

Mark McCord and his son, Aaron, were on a backpack summer fishing trip when they came upon the opportunity of-a-lifetime. They spotted Popeye summering in a high country basin. Mark decided to slip down and try to get some photos of the monster buck. There was only one small pine tree for cover as Mark moved slowly into the wind. Finally, the great mule deer was only 35 yards away feeding toward Mark as he snapped some unbelievable photos. Popeye moved within 20 yards before detecting Mark's presence and moving off. (Ref. pg. 183).

I have filmed some very large deer in Popeye's wintering area where it is not uncommon to see several 190-plus gross mule deer. Popeye is one, however, that I have been able to document throughout his mature years. (Ref to Chart). In my video Mule Deer Stalker III, you will see some up close footage of him taken over the last two years. It's unbelievable to see such a buck living in a general hunting area.

Eddie Boe, who has a degree in wildlife management from the University of Wyoming, estimates Popeye to be between seven and eight years old. Due to Wyoming's extremely harsh winters, our bucks usually don't live much beyond nine or 10 years, so this old buck will probably die of old age rather than a hunter's gun.

The Eastman videos, Mule Deer Stalker I and II, contain segments on antler development. They also document Popeye, as well as another huge buck that scores over 200 typical, as they continue to get older. This footage provides you with a look at the effect aging has on antler development.

1994/95
Gross nontypical
245 4/8
Photo by Dave Long

1994
Photo by Dave Long

1995-96
Gross nontypical
238

Photo by Jack Hone

1995 sheds

Photo by Alan Sinner

Photo by Mark McCord
1995

Photo by Mark McCord
1995

Eddie Boe holding Popeye's 1996-97 drops. He has successfully found four consecutive years of the buck's sheds giving us a rare glimpse at a huge mule deer's antler growth during his prime.

Popeye's

Gross Scores

Year	Typical score	Total nontypical inches	Nontypical score	Est. outside spread
1994-95	207 6/8	37 6/8	245 4/8	37
1995-96	220	18	238	37 7/8
1996-97	217 6/8	32 4/8	250 2/8	40

Chapter 19

Future of High Mountain Mule Deer Hunting

The high mountain mule deer is becoming a lost subspecies. All over the West their range is shrinking. It's not the summer range on public land that's being depleted, rather with the mass of human populations moving into the Rocky Mountain states their migration corridors are been gobbled up by development.

The affect on the migration corridors these deer use to get to the winter ranges is often drastic. Some of these deer will travel up to 70 miles over mountain ranges, major rivers and open country while rutting along the way. The southern Yellowstone elk herd travels 70 to 80 miles to the National Elk Refuge near Jackson Hole, Wyoming. It's probably one of the longest migration of a species in the lower 48 states. A straight shot through two national parks and a large national forest right near their feed grounds insures an open corridor for the elk migration.

This is not the case with many high mountain mule deer routes. Just the other day I was going over the rim where the Green River comes out of the Gros Ventre Range on highway 189 north of Pinedale Wyoming. Looking out across this large sage brush flat I could see newly constructed houses everywhere. They are standing right in the middle of the migration route of some of the best trophy mule herds in this part of the country. On the west side of the valley at the base of the mountain range, summer homes are gobbling up large tracts of ranch land that is also right in the middle of these deer migration routes. Some Game and Fish officials contend the deer will adjust their migration patterns, but I have lived around these deer for 43 years and it's not so!

Mule deer can't take the stress of people with their barking dogs, and the traffic that has suddenly increased 1,000 percent on the highways and county roads they have to cross. Go take a look at the Sage Junction road near the Wyoming and Utah border. Hundreds of the deer from the south part of the Salt River and Wyoming Ranges are hit by cars and semi trucks as they attempt to cross this major highway trying to get to their historical winter range. Hundreds of deer! Studies on winter range vegetation are ongoing, but little consideration is given to the study of migration routes.

The development of subdivisions on migration corridors has choked off historical routes between summer and winter range. Because of this,

I've seen the decline of mule deer in the Jackson Hole valley over the last 35 years. With golf courses and million dollar houses in front of them, mule deer have been reduced to a small portion of their earlier numbers. Gone are the many trophy deer that came across this stretch of country going to the buttes next to town. There will be some educated wildlife academe who would disagree, but they haven't spent 40 years watching the same deer herd. The best information they can draw on is only 20 year-old second-hand accounts.

A decade from now with the mass influx of people and subdivisions to the western corridors next to these picturesque mountain ranges, we will see the day when high mountain mule deer will become a rare sight. Like the plains grizzly bear, buffalo and other animals, the high mountain mule deer will fade into history. It is very sad for me after spending my life watching these noble deer in their summer and winter areas. They have a home range that can be 100 miles long going from summer to winter range. But guess what, no amount of imposed limited quota hunting management or conservation program is going to bring them back.

I believe we are seeing the beginnings of the latest movement of the United States affluent population as they try to catch the vanishing life style we have enjoyed here in the West. The sad part is, as they try to escape their social decay, they just bring it with them. Perhaps with some education and action we can stop the flood of people to these areas. Let's save at least a few of these special corridors that have historically been used by deer. It's the only way we are going to protect the last of these special mule deer.

Section V

Areas

Mike's High Country Area Picks

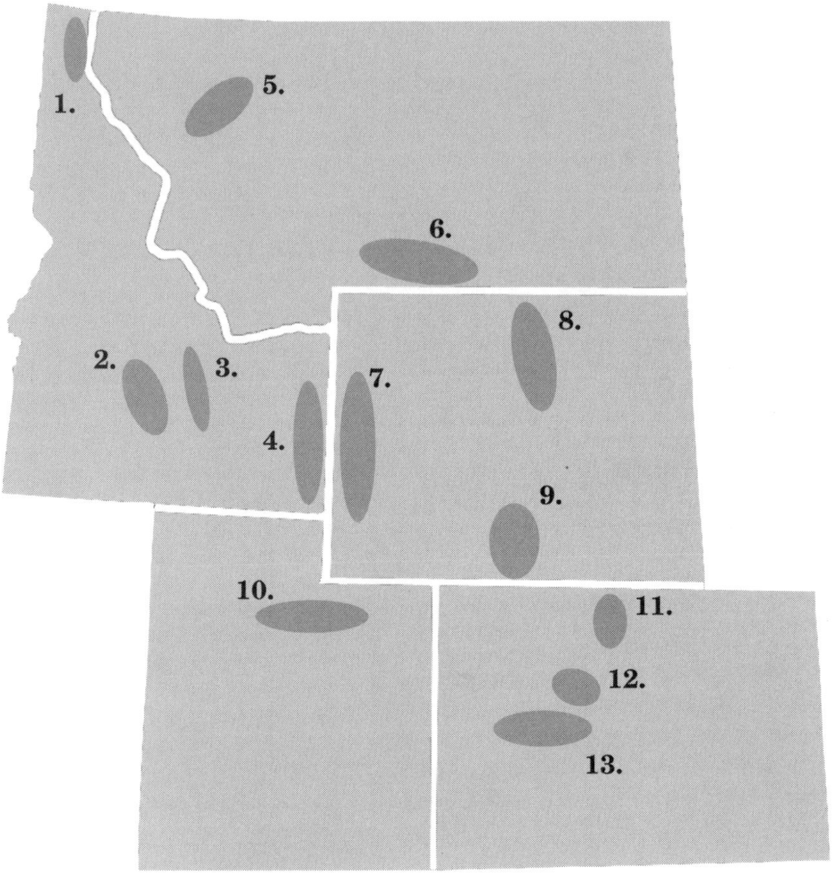

Idaho	1.	Kootnai
	2.	Sawtooth
	3.	Lost River Range
	4.	Caribou National Forest
Montana	5.	Unit 280 (Sept. Buck Hunt)
	6.	Unit 316 (Sept. High Country Hunt)
Wyoming	7.	Region G & H
	8.	Bighorns
	9.	Sierra Madre
Utah	10.	Kamas & North Slope (High Country Buck Hunts)
Colorado	11.	Unit 6, 7 - (High Country Rifle Hunts)
	12.	Unit 44, 45, 444 (High Country Rifle Hunts)
	13.	Unit 36 (High Country Rifle Hunts)

Tip: **These are a few of the best areas, but I encourage you to do your own research as well.**

Chapter 20

High Country Areas

If you hunt mule deer in the high country, then you probably already have your own special spots. Many guys, however, would like to learn more about high mountain mule deer areas. Several states offer high country hunting opportunities and I would like to share some of my personal thoughts about them. These suggestions should serve only as a starting point for you to begin your own research.

Idaho

The mountains of Idaho hold some of the best hidey holes for good deer. If you have ever taken a drive from Boise north to Granville right up through the heart of Idaho, you know what I mean. With its huge mountain ranges the state has many potential areas for trophy mule deer.

Southeastern Idaho is noted for big deer but after the bad winter of 92-93, this once-great area is struggling to come back to its full potential. However if you look farther north into some of the other mountain ranges of Idaho you can still find some good hunting.

Personally, I like the Sawtooth Range. It doesn't hold a lot of deer but in the past some good trophy bucks have come out of these mountains. Be advised, this country is extremely rugged. You must be in shape to tackle this mountain range.

The Lost River and Lemhi Ranges are other areas that can hold decent bucks. Over the years, the Owyhee Mountains south of Boise have been on a draw and the good bucks are finally coming back. At one time it was common to find non-typicals in this area but because of over hunting it's been a long road back for the recovery of trophy mule deer. The Salmon River country has been noted for large bucks, but it is a tough area to hunt. The terrain is straight up and down with very few trails.

The northern panhandle has a couple of early fall draw areas that can produce good results. Some of the state's late season, limited draw areas have bucks that migrate in from the surrounding mountains.

Overall, Idaho is one state I think will produce some good high mountain hunting. Do your research and find a good area. Their general licenses are on first come, limited quota for nonresident and you need to apply in late December. They even have a system where you can call in and pay for your license with a credit card. Because the good tags go fast first, don't wait until January or you'll miss out.

Wyoming

My home state has great high mountain hunting. The western sections in region H and G are noted for big deer, but other Wyoming mountain ranges are often overlooked.

The Snowy Range is one good area that comes to mind. It is a little hard to find access but if you can get back into the area, it holds big deer. In the 60s and 70s, some giant bucks came out of the high country basins of the Snowy Range.

The Bighorns are not well known for big bucks but I have seen some real good deer on its winter range. This mountain range can be hard to hunt because the season is in October and by then the snow has pushed many of the deer down into the thick timber stands. The Bighorns contain many lodge pole pine tree stands that run for miles. Once a big buck gets in to one of these, he just hides out waiting for the rut. Don't let this discourage you, because if you poke around I think you will end up finding a high mountain pocket full of bucks. If the snows come later in October these bucks could still be hanging around up high during the first week of the season.

Some of the best mule deer hunting in Wyoming is found in the wilderness where nonresidents are required to hire a guide. The Gros Ventre and Teton mountain ranges are two that fall into this category. There are some good outfitters in both of these areas that specialize in mule deer hunting. They always take a few monster bucks each year.

Some other areas worth looking at are down in the Sierra Madre Range along the Colorado border or one of my favorites, the Snake River Range on the Idaho-Wyoming border.

Wyoming is on a draw by region and in some of the popular areas like region G and H it is hard to get a permit. That is one reason I have listed these other areas that aren't nearly as hard to draw for. Most guys overlook them in favor of the more high profile units.

As of this writing, Wyoming's high country holds some of the best trophy mule deer in the country. The main reason is Wyoming's game management policy of allowing only a few nonresident tags combined with the low population of the state. To give you an example, I live in the least populated county in the least populated state. This combination makes for great hunting and wildlife filming opportunities.

Colorado

More big deer have come from Colorado than any other state. Unfortunately, for the last 20 years it has been over-hunted. With hundreds of thousands of hunters each year, the deer have suffered a drastic decrease. You can purchase over-the-counter mule deer permits, but I don't hunt the general season on public land there. Colorado has large and high mountain ranges, but by the time the mid-October three- or five-day general season arrives, most of the bucks have pulled out of the high country. On an average year the snows have pushed them down off the high basins and ridges to the timber where it's almost impossible to hunt them. During the general hunting season if you can hit a dry year and hunt up high, you will find some bucks still hanging out hiding from hunters in rugged basins or steep slides.

If you are interested in high mountain mule deer hunting you must check out this state's early season areas. These are high mountain draw hunts that require only one or two preference points. By doing your homework, you can find an area that will produce for you in September. It's high altitude hunting, (sometimes above 12,000 feet), but with only a few permits available the quality of hunting in these units is great. I like to hunt along the Wyoming border during these early hunts.

I hope Colorado's Game Department will wise up and start managing their deer herds for quality. For now, however, it seems the revenue dollars outweigh having a good healthy deer population. Don't give up on Colorado, it still has the best history for big bucks.

Montana

Recently, Montana has been trying to implement a new mule deer plan. After decades of hunting seasons that run during the rut there are very few public land areas in Montana with good buck to doe ratios. The Achilles heel of a mule deer buck is the rut when he gets dumb and throws caution to the wind. I guarantee you will kill most of your mature bucks if hunting is allowed during this period.

A while back I was shown some bucks taken in Montana on well-managed private property. I had to admit, Montana has good genetics just bad mule deer management.

It is possible find some early, high mountain draw hunts in Montana. If you stop and look at these, I bet you can come up with a good trophy area. Stay away from areas that have early elk seasons that run with the deer season.

I personally haven't hunted Montana, but I feel it's worth looking at. If they cut back the permits and set their hunting season before the rut, in five years I know they could have some good mule deer hunting.

This is why it is so important to be on the leading edge of what is happening in the various mule deer states. If a new plan is going to be implemented by the game and fish that will benefit the propagation of trophy deer, you need to be aware of it. That way you can plan your hunt well in advance.

Utah

This state has produced some very big bucks in the past, but the 92-93 winter kill really slowed down the northern areas. The Game and Fish have put the state on a draw and cut the number of licenses back to about what they were in the early 70s. In the long run this will help the deer population immensely.

Utah is another state that has early draw hunts in the high country. You don't hear much about the success, but I think it can't do anything but get better. This providing a bad winter doesn't come in and leave a big die-off. Utah is noted more for desert deer than high mountain hunting. However if you look at the Wasatch and Uinta Mountains, there are some high peaks, nice basins and slides that are conducive to this type of hunting.

Photo by Jim Van Norman